SINGWOOD
AND ORIES

Guess the endings

*Selected and brought within the 1800 word vocabulary
of New Method Supplementary Reader, Stage 5, by*

MICHAEL WEST

Illustrated by Harry Green

LONGMAN

LONGMAN GROUP LIMITED
London

*Associated companies, branches and representatives
throughout the world*

This edition © Longman Group Ltd 1963

*First published 1963
New impressions *1965 (twice) ;
*1966; *1967; *1969 (twice) ; *1970;
*1972 (twice) ; *1974 (twice)
1976 (with Corrections)*

ISBN 0 582 53491 7

Note:
Words with a star* are outside stage 5 of the
New Method Supplementary Readers and are not
explained in the text. These extra words are in a list
on page 104.

*Printed in Hong Kong by
Dai Nippon Printing Co. (H.K.) Ltd.*

Foreword

The Short Story builds up quickly to a climax and then usually ends in a very unexpected way.

These stories have been selected as being most suitable to the foreign reader and most provocative to anyone trying to predict the ending.

A note in italics shows where the reader may stop reading and try to guess the ending of the story which, in every case, is given on the following page.

iii

Acknowledgements

We are grateful to the following for permission to include copyright material.

Mrs. L. G. Barnard for an adaptation of The Red Fish-Cart, originally called *The Yellow Fish-Cart*, by the late L. G. Barnard; the authors' agents for adaptations of *Lady in the Dark* by Victor Canning and "Secret Agent", originally called *The Desperate Mission of Su Mei*, by Mark Derby; Doubleday & Co. Inc. for adaptations of The Gifts of the Magi from *The Four Million*, and One Thousand Dollars from *Voice of the City* by O. Henry, reprinted by permission; the Trustees of the late Dr. R. Austen Freeman and Hodder & Stoughton Ltd. for an adaptation of The Blue Scarab from *Dr. Thorndyke's Casebook*; Muriel Jemmett for an adaptation of Past and Future, originally called *Back to the Future*; the author and William Heinemann Ltd. for an abridged and adapted version of The Luncheon from *Cosmopolitans* by W. Somerset Maugham; the literary representatives of Stephen Phillips for an adaptation of *Nearer to God than Gold*; the literary representatives of the late John Russell for an adaptation of *The Fourth Man*; Patricia Sibley for an adaptation of The Better Way, originally called *The Colour of Happiness*; and the author's agents for an adaptation of *Singing Wind* by J. D. Sleightholme.

Contents

"Keep your hand off that gun."

Nearer to God than Gold

Adapted from a story by Stephen Phillips

Jesse was almost at the top of the hill when he heard the shot. He looked upwards: in the evening light all that he could see was dark shapes; then he saw a *mule* with an old man sitting on it. As he looked, the old man fell sideways and lay still in the dust. Jesse did not move, but his hand felt for the pistol hanging at his side. The old man lay dead. Then the two killers came in sight. One was a big man but very thin: the other was very short and fat. Shortie (the short man) had a gun in his hand. They looked down and saw Jesse.

"He's only a boy; leave him," said the thin man.

"Yes," said Shortie; "only a boy, as you say; but a boy has eyes, like everyone else!"

Jesse's brown hand was touching his pistol. He was only eighteen years old, but that brown hand knew as much about pistol-shooting as many a trained soldier.

"Keep your hand off that gun," said Shortie, "and come up here."

The boy climbed up, keeping his eyes fixed on them. He stood breathless in front of them.

"Yes, he's got eyes," said the thin man. "So has the lady down there; but she wouldn't notice a monkey riding on a white donkey."

Shortie laughed.

Jesse looked down: 'The Lady?' What lady? What did he mean when he said that she wouldn't notice 'a monkey riding on a white donkey'? Why had they shot the old man? In anger? Or because he carried something which they wanted?

"You've seen a man killed before, haven't you, boy?" said Shortie.

"Yes. I saw my father killed, at Devil's Rock, standing with his hands empty, as I'm standing now."

"You've seen what happened, and you'll talk—eh?"

"I'm not the talking kind."

Jesse felt them looking at him. The boy's face told them nothing; it was hard, square, burnt by the desert sun, dirty. He hadn't washed for days: in those places there was too little water to waste on washing. What he said was true: he had seen his father killed looking for gold. In this desert most men died in that way—looking for gold. Perhaps he would die in that way too, but he didn't feel afraid; he was wondering why they did it. Why did they shoot that old man? They had not looked in the old man's pockets or in the bags hanging on the mule, so as to find anything. Then why? Why —— ?

Just then the mule kicked: its feet caught Shortie and sent him rolling down the hillside. Jesse watched the mule; it went off along the dry bed of a stream. The thin man pulled out his gun, but he did not shoot. Why not? Shortie was climbing up the hill. The thin man turned to Jesse. "All right, boy; run! Before the mule gets back—and don't talk!"

Jesse ran. He knew now what they wanted: it was the mule. But why?

He followed the mule. As he went on, he saw just below him a small wooden building. The door opened and he saw the shape of a woman—or was it a girl? He came nearer: she wasn't pretty; her face and hair were covered with the dirt and dust of the place. She wasn't looking towards him. There was something strange in the way she stood there: she seemed to be looking upwards at—nothing! The mule was standing in the dark shadow of the house.

Jesse moved: she turned her face towards him.

"Who are you?" she asked. "What do you want?"

"My name's Jesse—Jesse Lyne."

He came closer: his feet turned up the dust as he moved. Now he understood what was meant by the 'monkey riding on a white donkey' . . . The Lady was blind.

He didn't know what to say: he felt so sorry for her. Blind—in this desert. It must be terrible.

"Dear old Lucifer!" Her voice was very gentle. Her hand touched the mule's neck. "I knew you would come back if you could. . . . I heard the shot," she said.

"Yes." The boy spoke slowly and carefully. "It was up there, on the hill-top." He stopped: he felt that she was afraid, not for herself although she was blind, but for some other reason. He didn't want to make that fear greater. He was dirty and smelly, and his blood was hot and wild, but he felt sorry for her—deeply sorry. "You mustn't be afraid, Lady. Perhaps the old man didn't feel any pain."

"Old man? Do you mean that he was attacked?"

"Yes," he said, " . . . Yes."

"That old man stole Lucifer. Donald—that's my brother —saw him from the window: he spends a lot of time just looking out of the window."

There were so many questions that Jesse wanted to ask, but in the desert one learns not to ask too many questions. He felt that the Lady was in some way different from the other women he knew. Her voice was soft. In the lamplight shining from the doorway he saw only the dark shape of her, but she seemed finer—different from the others.

"I wonder why the mule was stolen, Lady," said Jesse, "Mules aren't worth much: they don't cost much money."

"Lucifer isn't like other mules," she said.

He followed her inside. She left the door open. She called loudly: "Maquita!" He saw a fat dark woman, a Mexican-Indian. "Maquita, take Lucifer away and feed her."

"*Si, senorita*" (Yes, lady); but the boy moved more quickly. "I'll do it, Lady."

He had some difficulty in getting the mule into the hut; then he climbed up to the top of the hill and lay there, watching. The desert seemed empty, but he knew that it was not so. Someone was there, waiting.

He went back to the house. Maquita brought food to the table. As he ate Jesse was thinking deeply, taking little notice of the Lady. Her face was small and covered with dirt and dust. Her hair was a sort of dirty golden colour, tied up with bits of string.

Jesse hardly looked at her as she sat there at the table, yet he felt sure that she was glad that he had stayed.

He wondered what had happened to her brother. As he went past an open door he had seen a young man lying flat on his back on a bed; his eyes were shut. The girl seemed to read Jesse's thoughts. "Donald can't walk," she said. "It happened near Flagstone soon after we came here—nearly a year ago. An explosion came too soon."

Jesse understood: they had been using an explosive in getting gold out of the rocks.

"Gold! Gold!" she cried. "Why do men go down on their knees to gold? . . . as if it was a god, and give their lives for it?"

The meal was finished: they left the table. Jesse stood, looking at her: his mouth was wide open with surprise.

"But . . . but why shouldn't men look for gold? It's the most valuable thing there is."

She turned as if to look at him: "Jesse, how old are you?"

"How old?" he said. "That's a strange thing to ask me. No woman ever asked me that before. I think I'm about eighteen."

They were now standing quite close to each other. Jesse had been travelling for weeks in the dry, waterless desert: he carried with him the smell of those unwashed places.

"Jesse," she said, "you seem to think that there's nothing quite so important as gold—don't you? Well, let me tell you that there are things which are far, far more important.

Cleanness is one of them. Didn't anyone ever tell you of the saying, 'Cleanliness* is next to godliness'?"

He was so surprised that he could find no answer.

"Over there by the door, Jesse, we keep a pot full of water for use in case of any great need. I think this is one."

He began to understand.

"What!" he said, "—waste water in that way, Lady—in washing!"

It was as if she had asked him to do some terribly wrong thing. He had been born in the desert: he had lived all his life in the desert where every cupful of water was counted: a cupful of water might be a matter of life or death. But he did what she said.

When he had finished she used the last few cupfuls of water to wash away the dust from her own face and neck.

"Tell me about those two men whom you saw on the hill tonight," she said. "I think they are the men who came here two days ago. My brother saw them."

Jesse did not want to tell her the truth.

"I think they've gone away by now," he said. "Why do you stay here? Why don't you go away?"

"It's my brother," she answered. "He's always hoping. He's sure that his legs will be all right again, and that then he'll find gold here, as my father, Doctor Charlie, did. So I have to stay. I couldn't leave him, could I?"

Jesse remembered the name of Doctor Charlie: his story was well known.

"This place belonged to Doctor Charlie. He was shot dead one night coming back with the mule. He went into the hills with the mule every day when he had found the gold. In the end the mule could lead him to the place, like a dog leading a blind man. That's why they want the mule—to lead them to the place, to Doctor Charlie's gold. But really it's quite foolish because there's no gold left. It was all cleaned out before he died."

* The first step towards being good is to keep yourself clean.

"If that's so, Lady, why don't you let them take the mule?"

She did not answer. Her silence made him wonder if she had been speaking the truth. Was the gold really "all cleaned out"?

The night passed. Jesse waited and watched.

Just before the sun came up he heard the sound which he had been waiting for—feet in the dust outside. He opened the door, and there he saw the two killers.

"What's the matter, boy?" asked the thin man. "Can't you sleep?"

"Don't come any nearer," said Jesse quietly. "I've got a gun."

"Little boy, we aren't meaning to hurt anyone. We know that the Lady is blind: so the old mule takes her to the place up there. We've seen her go, once every week. But she doesn't leave any footmarks that we can follow: it's hard rock up there. . . ."

"Get away from here," said Jesse. "Go!"

They went and there was an ugly look in their eyes.

Jesse gave an angry laugh. Why hadn't the Lady spoken the truth when he was only trying to help her? The gold was not "all cleaned out"; it was still there.

Next night Jesse watched from a window. He saw the Lady walking beside the mule.

"She went out of the back door," he thought angrily, "so that I shouldn't see."

Then he saw the two men following her. Moving very quietly, he followed them. He was sure now of the reason why the Lady and her brother were staying down here in the heat and dirt. Yet he could not leave her in danger from those men.

They went up and up. The rocks were hard now—like glass; no marks of feet were left on them. Then they went down again on the other side. Then, as he looked up at the

The rock came rolling down the hill

hillside opposite, he saw the Lady and the mule going along a narrow pathway, only a few feet wide. The mule was in front, and the Lady had one hand on his back. Jesse was filled with wonder how a blind woman could be so brave when one wrong step would throw her down to her death.

Then he saw something—the face of the short man just above him. He was pushing a great piece of rock, almost as big as himself. As the rock came rolling and jumping down the hill, Jesse threw himself to one side, and at the same second he fired. He heard a cry and the man fell. Then the big man fired shot after shot, and Jesse fired back at him. A bit of rock hit Jesse's face: he felt the blood. The big man was turning round and round as if he were dancing: then he fell.

Jesse jumped up and ran like a mad thing along that narrow pathway. He came to a thin crack in the wall of rock, hidden until one was very close to it. He went through. The crack became wider and he came out into the open, under the sky of early morning.

This was the place!

This was the place where Doctor Charlie had found gold. He could see the marks where explosive had been used to break out the gold-bearing rock. He examined it: the Lady was right: all the gold had gone; it had been worked out. Not a bit remained.

The anger in his heart died. He laughed. Then his mind was filled with one great question: Why? Why? If there was no gold, why did she come here, week after week? Why?

You may stop reading here and try to guess the end. Why did the Lady go there if there was no gold? Or was there gold?

He heard the Lady calling from below and he shouted back, his young voice ringing through the clear cold air: "It's all right, Lady. It's me—Jesse!"

"Jesse? Oh! I thought . . . . But what brings you here; and what was that shooting?"

"Some animal; among the rocks."

He looked down. The mule was standing there, waiting. There, also, the Lady stood; but she was different from the Lady that he remembered seeing back in the desert and dirt and heat; here was a new and shining Lady.

"You may come down, Jesse."

He went down slowly, and with every step he took, his wonder grew. For this she had come within a step of death! She had endangered her life for this!

Her hair was not tied up now with bits of string; it lay loose. She was pulling on her high boots.

Jesse stopped just a few steps in front of her. She seemed to read his thoughts. "Yes, Jesse, it's quite all right for you to have a bath in front of a blind girl. Here's the soap."

2

"Secret Agent"

Adapted from "The Desperate Mission of Su Mei", by Mark Derby

An agent* is a person used to do something for another person. For example, a secret agent is a person who does secret work for a government.

Was this child a secret agent carrying some message from the enemy in that other country across the river? And yet she was shot by their soldiers just as she swam across the river. What was the message which she was carrying?

* * * *

The doctor stepped back and looked down at the woman lying there on the table. No, she was not a woman, only a child near to womanhood. The shot had passed right through the body and had been taken out above the right breast.

"She was very young for this sort of thing," said the nurse.

"Yes," said the doctor. "She was in the river when they shot her. She was almost across, all but a few yards."

He thought angrily of the darkness and the cold river—the men called out from the police post, then firing through the starlight, and the girl pulling herself up onto the shore and getting into some bushes where the soldiers on this side found her in the first light of day.

The nurse raised the left arm of the girl. "What about this?" she asked. On the underside of the upper arm there was a small roll, covered to protect it from the water. "Perhaps you'd better take care of this for the present." She gave it to the doctor.

"An agent," said the doctor. "An agent?" At that age? And yet if she was not an agent something very important must have driven her to do such a dangerous thing."

The doctor put the roll in his pocket, then he went out into the garden for a smoke. For a moment he stood smelling the sweet red roses of which the nurse was so proud. He took the little roll out of his pocket and took off the outside cover. Inside it he found a long piece of red silk, deep red, red as blood. Words had been stitched* with a needle onto it, each letter made up of hundreds of very small stitches. He could not read the strange writing. He rolled it up again and put it back in his pocket.

Late that afternoon the nurse came to him: "That girl, Su Mei, has missed the thing which was tied on her arm, and now she's getting very anxious about it. Will you see her? She speaks English very well."

He went along to her. Her eyes looked up at him, eager and anxious. "Are you the doctor who took the shot out of my body? You stole from me! The fat nurse told me."

He took out the little roll: "I kept this safe for you." He handed it to her.

Her eyes filled with tears. "Thank you—I ask your forgiveness," she said. "I am very sorry." Tears ran down her face.

Why did this little thing cause such deep feeling. Peace was what the child needed. She must be made to think of something else.

"Where did you learn to speak English so well?" he asked.

"From Miss Rosa," she said. He felt as if this name was a sign of peace and trust.

"She taught you and your sisters?"

"I have no sisters or brothers or father or mother: Miss Rosa was the teacher in the Children's Home. I lived there with the other children who had no family. Everybody loved her. We called her Miss Rosa because she was so fond of

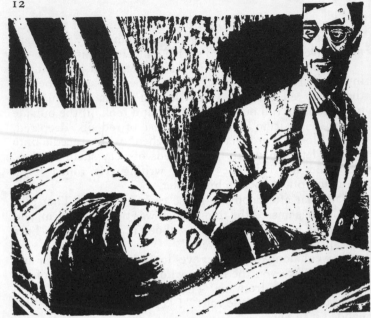

"I kept this safe for you."

roses. She planted them. The rose-bush near the Paper Boat bridge was the best."

He let her talk. It seemed to calm her.

"We started the paper boat races from that bridge. The winner was given a sweet, and the loser was given some work to do."

She smiled for the first time. "But Miss Rosa always knew who would win. I was the only one who found out what she did. The child who won was always someone who had been sad or in trouble, or someone who had a birthday that day. The one who lost was someone who had been bad: a bad child never won."

She shut her eyes: she was beginning to feel sleepy.

"You see, the stream was faster on one side than on the other, and Miss Rosa always arranged the boats in line herself. I won on my birthday. . . . Miss Rosa loved birthdays."

"Thank you for telling me all this," said the doctor. "Now you must go to sleep."

"Shall I be better tomorrow?" she asked.

"Yes," he said, "yes, if you sleep."

* * * *

"She's gone!" said the nurse next morning. "She has gone away—with that hole right through her! She said, 'The doctor told me that I would be better today and I have something very important to do.' I told her not to be silly; but when I came back she had gone."

Next day Su Mei was brought back by the police. She was put into bed and given hot drinks. As soon as she was a little better she was given something to make her sleep.

The doctor saw her again that night.

"Why did they bring me back again?" she whispered. She was very weak. Then after a time she asked, "What day is this?" He told her.

She seized his hand. "You must help me," she said. "You must! . . . Will you help me?"

"Is it about that thing which you had under your arm?"

"Yes," she said. "I would not ask for myself. I didn't come all this way for myself; I am a . . . ."

"An agent," he said. "Are you an agent?"

"Yes, an agent. I must do what I am sent to do. I must do it today."

"You mean, it's a message? Can I take it for you?"

"I am so afraid that I am too late." Her eyes were filled with tears.

"Just tell me where I have to take it, and I'll go now."

"But I don't know!" she cried. "I didn't know that this city was so big. Yesterday I asked many people; then one of them said that she would help me, but she went to the telephone; and so I ran away. Will you find Miss Rosa for me? Please, please find Miss Rosa!"

She was only a child now, a small child. She turned to him as if to the father whom she had never known, the father who takes charge of all baby anxieties and troubles.

"Don't be afraid," he said. "We'll find her."

"But today!" she said. "Today! Find her today! She is here. When the new government sent all the teachers away, Miss Rosa was too ill to go to Europe with the others, so she stayed there with us. Then after a long time she became very ill and they sent her across the river. . . . They sent her here. Miss Rosa is here in this city."

"I'm going to call a friend on the telephone," he said. When he came back she was still very troubled and anxious.

"It's all right," he said. "I can take you to Miss Rosa."

The joy which shone in her eyes was something which he would remember all his life.

"Today?"

"Now. We'll get a wheel-chair for you."

As he pushed the chair out of the door she turned with eyes like stars and said: "On the way I must buy some roses. She loves them. I have money."

He said, "Just a minute."

Soon he was back, looking rather ashamed, and he had in his hand four red roses from the bush that the nurse was so proud of.

He wheeled the chair along to another part of the hospital. Then he opened the door: "A visitor for you, Miss Rosa."

You may stop reading here and try to guess the ending. What was the message? How or why was Su Mei chosen to take it?

It was a very small room full of sunlight. Sitting up on a bed was a very old woman.

"Dear Miss Rosa," said Su Mei. "I have come to bring you some roses and a message."

"You! God bless you, my child! Roses!" She took them in her thin white fingers.

"Read the message," said Su Mei.

The old woman whispered the words as she read them:

"A greeting on her eightieth birthday to dear Miss Rosa whom we loved from our youngest years and will love always until we are as old as she is."

Then followed twenty-eight names, each stitched by its owner's hand.

"But, my child, you look ill," said Miss Rosa.

"No, no, the doctor has made me well. There were some bad policemen and I had to swim across the river."

Miss Rosa closed her eyes at the thought of the terrible danger. Then at last she took up the piece of silk again.

"How was it that you were chosen to bring me this wonderful gift?"

"We made paper boats, Miss Rosa, as you taught us when we were little, and we raced them in the stream."

"Ah, my poor child! And you lost?"

The girl looked up at the doctor with a smile.

"No, Miss Rosa," she said. "I won."

3
One Thousand Dollars

Adapted from a story by O. Henry

"One thousand dollars," said the lawyer, coldly; "and here is the money." He had not a very good opinion of Richard Waring; he did not like him.

Richard Waring laughed as he took the thin packet of notes. "It's difficult to know what to do with just one thousand dollars. Of course, I could go to a fine hotel and live like a prince for a few days; or I could give up my work in the office and do what I want to do—paint pictures: I could do that for a few weeks. But what would I do after that? I should have lost my place in the office, and have no money to live on. If it were a little less money, I would buy a new coat or a radio, or give a dinner to my friends. If it were more, I could give up the work in the office and paint pictures. But it's too much for one and too little for the other."

"You heard the reading of your uncle's Will*," said the lawyer, "telling what is to be done with his money after his death. I must ask you to remember one point. Your uncle has said that you must bring me a paper showing exactly what you did with this money, as soon as you have spent it. That is your uncle's wish, as written in his Will. I hope you will do as he asked."

"Yes, I'll do it," said the young man.

Richard wasn't a bad young man, or a foolish young man; but he did not like working in an office. What he really loved was painting pictures. He was a good painter; but there's no money in painting pictures. What was the use of saving? Whenever he got a present from his rich uncle he spent it.

inherit
in wealth

So the rich uncle said, "He's a young fool and does not know how to use money."

Richard Waring went along to his friend Old Bryson. He found him half-asleep over a newspaper.

"I've just come from my uncle's lawyer," said Richard. "He has left me just one thousand dollars, and when I've spent it I have to tell the lawyer what I did with it. What can a man do with just one thousand dollars—no more, no less?"

"I thought that your uncle was a very rich man, worth half a million."

"He was," said Richard, "but he hasn't left it to me. He has left $100 and a gold ring to each of his servants, and $1000 to me. And I expect all the rest goes to a hospital or something like that. . . . What can one do with $1000?". .

"Is there no other person to whom the money might go? Hadn't he any family?" asked Bryson.

Richard did not answer at once; then he said, "There's Mary Hayden, the daughter of a friend of my uncle. She lived in his house, and she got $100 and a gold ring—like the rest of the servants. I wish I'd had just that—just $100 and a ring. I would have had a good dinner with my friends and that would have been the end of it. Now, don't tell me I'm a fool, but tell me what can a man do with $1000?"

Old Bryson took off his glasses and rubbed them.

"One thousand dollars," he said, "may mean much—or little. One man might buy a home with it—just a hut, yet to him a home. Another man might get the best doctor and treatment for his sick wife. It would pay for sending a clever boy to a day-school for a few years; or it could be lost in a few seconds at Monte Carlo. It would buy a fine picture—or a bright jewel, or pay for printing a learned book if it wasn't too big."

"I did not ask you to give me a lesson, but to tell me how to spend $1000. What would you do?"

"There's only one thing you can do. Give the money as a

present to some poor person who will use it well and get a lot of happiness out of it. And, having done that, just forget it and go on living as you did before."

Richard Waring stood outside Bryson's house thinking. "'Give it to someone who will use it well and get happiness out of it.' I might buy a jewel for some beautiful woman. Clara Lane who is singing at the theatre is beautiful—but the jewels which she wears are worth thousands: she would get no happiness from a thousand-dollar ring. I might give it to the doorman at the office. I asked him once what he would do if he had money; he wants to open a drink-shop; that's not using money well. I might give it to the blind man who sits asking for money in the Square, but people give him so much that I'm sure he has more than $1000 in the bank: he doesn't need it."

Richard got onto a bus and went back to the lawyer's office.

"Tell me," he said: "did my uncle leave anything to Miss Hayden beside the $100 and the gold ring?"

"Nothing," said the lawyer.

Richard went to his uncle's house. Miss Hayden was still there. She was sitting writing a letter. She turned over the paper and put her hand on it when she saw Richard.

"I've just come from the lawyer," he said. "He has been going over the papers: he found something added to the Will—an after-thought. My uncle left you $1000. Here it is. You'd better count it and see that it's right."

He put the money on the table.

"Oh!" she cried.

"I wish . . . ." he said. "I want . . . ." He stopped. He looked at her—her dear sweet face and kind eyes. Then he looked round the beautiful room, the wealth and richness of it, and thought of his poor little home far outside the town. It wouldn't be any use asking her to marry him; she wouldn't be happy.

He hurried away.

"This paper was given to me by your uncle."

Richard went back to the lawyer's office, and wrote on a piece of paper, "Paid by Richard Waring one thousand dollars to the best and dearest woman in the world, knowing that no one will use the money better or get more happiness from it."

He went into the lawyer's room.

"I've spent the money," he said; "and I've written a note on this paper showing what I did with it. . . . It's a nice bright day, isn't it; quite a beautiful spring day!"

Without taking the paper, the lawyer stood up and went out of the room. After a few minutes he came back carrying a large paper.

"Mr. Waring," he said, solemnly, "this paper was given to me by your uncle: he ordered me not to read it until you had used the $1000 and had told me, in writing, on what you had spent it. This paper says that, if in spending the money you have shown yourself wise and unselfish, I am to give you $100,000. But if the money has been spent foolishly, that money, $100,000, is to be paid to Mary Hayden, daughter of his friend. I will now read what you have written."

He put out his hand to take the paper but Richard was a little quicker in taking it up and putting it in his pocket.

"You needn't read it," he said. "I lost most of the money at the racecourse and I spent the rest on a dinner and drinks."

"Foolish, foolish young man!" said the lawyer, sadly.

You may stop reading here and try to guess the ending?
Who got the money? Did Richard marry Mary?

"I want to see Mr. Waring," said Mary. "He works in this office. I have a letter for him."

Richard came out from the door of the room where he worked and found Mary Hayden waiting to see him.

"Richard," she said, "I was just writing a letter to you when you came to see me. You had better read it now that I've finished it."

> "Dear Richard,
> Now that your uncle is dead, I am free to do what I want to do. I know that you want me to marry you; but you won't ask me because you think that I'm afraid of being the wife of a poor man. Dear Richard, I'm not afraid—if you aren't afraid of being married to a poor woman who loves you, as I know that you love me.
>
> . . . MARY"

"I told the lawyer what you did," said Mary. "So I'm still poor. I've got nothing—except $100."

4
The Red Fish-Cart

Adapted from a story by Leslie Gordon Barnard

I was a boy at the time, but I can still remember the feeling of mystery and terror around me during that holiday at the sea. I can remember sitting on the floor listening to my elders talking about a girl named Jeanne Adams, whose body was found down by the cliff. I remember that, later, the name of Millie Jones came into their talk.

Millie helped with the housework in old Angus's house. Angus was a fisherman, and my father and mother took lodgings in his house. She wasn't pretty: she was rather ugly. She was, as I know now, one of those wonderfully good people, those people who in their quiet way do so much good in the world.

Each day she drove her red cart down to the sea and brought back a load of fish for the market.

Old Angus had a daughter named Sophie. I think Sophie must have been very pretty: Millie said that she was. I think Millie knew that there would not be any love and marriage in her life, and that is why she was so interested in hearing about Sophie's young men. There were quite a lot of these until Joe Green came. Joe was the last one, and they loved each other very much. Joe had first gone about with Jeanne Adams, but she had a quarrel with him. Millie and I did not imagine at that time how dark a shadow that quarrel would cast over Joe and Sophie, or how at the end Millie was to be mixed up in it so strangely.

Even now I can remember the terror which came into me when people talked about Jeanne Adams and what had happened to her. They always talked in whispers about that;

but they spoke quite loud and openly about Joe Green and his part in it.

I asked Millie why this was, but all she said was, "Joe would never do such a terrible thing; but people know that he quarrelled with her. Hardy and Sholtz found him kneeling by the body. That was bad. And it was worse when Joe ran away. He should have stayed. I hope he'll come back himself before they go and fetch him."

Millie had her wish. Joe came back.

I remember the night well, with rain coming in from the sea, and a strong wind. He was wet and cold when he reached old Angus's back door. I had gone out to see about my fishing things and I almost ran into them. There was Sophie with her arms round Joe's neck and Joe was saying, "You don't believe it of me, do you?" And Sophie just shook her head, and then laid her head on his wet shoulder.

Joe said, "It's true that I was with Jeanne that evening, but it just happened that I met her on the road and we walked along together. We went past Hardy's place and Sholtz's hut, and then I turned off alone and let her go on. I went and lay in the grass above the cliff and wished that you were there with me. Then it got darker and the stars came out, and then —then I heard the cry. I ran, and after a time I found her. That is why I was kneeling beside her body when Hardy and Sholtz came to see if anything was wrong. That's the truth, Sophie."

Joe gave himself up to the police that night and I heard that he was in prison in the neighbouring town. I asked Millie if they would hang Joe Green, and then she looked frightened and said I mustn't talk like that.

Millie was strange in some ways. I said my prayers in the way any child has been taught to say them. But Millie just talked to God as if He was in the room. I heard her talking when I passed her bedroom door.

"We've got to do something about Sophie and Joe," she was saying. "They're nice people and they love each other

24

just as You want people to love each other, but they're in terrible trouble. We've got to do something.'' That's the way she talked to God.

Of course Hardy and Sholtz were the two most important people in the trial. The trial lasted two days and on both days there was heavy rain and a strong wind as if the weather was trying to make it hard for Joe. I could see by the way people talked and shook their heads, and by the look on Millie's face that things were going badly.

Now in any trial there are twelve jurymen*. The jurymen listen to what is said and they decide whether they think the case is proved. In this trial the jurymen had to decide whether it had been proved that Joe killed Jeanne—or not.

One of the jurymen was taken ill, and so the trial had to be stopped for two days. I heard the girls talking about it.

"I can't bear it, Millie," said Sophie. "I can't bear the waiting."

But Millie said, "Listen, Sophie. I've been praying very hard for you and Joe. Perhaps it was God who made this man fall ill. You never know!"

I wanted to laugh at the idea of God making a man fall ill because of Millie; but Sophie only cried.

Next day the sun came out, and it felt good after the wind and rain. The sea was bright, and I went out for a walk.

I went past the market where every day Millie came with her cart and the fish from the sea. I went past the church and the Town Hall and Dr. Gunter's house. Everywhere people were talking about the trial, and you could almost see the rope round Joe's neck.

I went along the shore, thinking how Joe had come this way on that terrible night. I could see the road going past Hardy's house where there were many children's clothes hanging out to dry, and past Sholtz's house where his nets were drying. Then I saw that the boats were coming in and the women and girls were going down to help with the fish which the men had caught. Just as I got there I saw Millie's red cart, bright in the sunlight. It was shining red because she had just repainted it. I'd often asked Millie why she didn't paint it, and now she had, but she hadn't oiled the wheels.

"I am going to see them land the fish," I told her.

I didn't get into the cart but I walked behind, because I had on a new suit of clothes, and I was afraid that the new paint on the cart might mark my clothes. When we got to the place where they were landing the fish, the sunlight had faded and the clouds were low, making a fog* over the sea.

When Angus saw me he said, "Now don't you get dirty, young fellow, or your mother will be angry with me." So I sat down at a little distance and watched them. Soon they began to talk about Joe Green, and I wished they wouldn't.

One after another the boats came in, and the last one to come in was Sholtz's boat. I can see him now standing up in his boat and throwing the fish onto the land. I kept looking at him and at Hardy and thinking how they had found Joe kneeling by Jeanne Adams's body.

"Sholtz doesn't want to be married," said someone, "and have all his money go on the children's clothes and food— like Hardy. He says, 'I keep a sharp watch on myself. I want to stay as I am.'"

The daylight faded and the fog became thicker. I was cold,

so I walked along the shore and then came back again. When I came back they were talking about Joe.

Sholtz was saying, "I don't want to hear any more of this. If Joe is hanged—and I think he will be—it's because he's done what he has done, not because of Hardy and me. There was nothing we could do but speak the truth about it."

Hardy said, "Of course, in a court of law you must speak the truth."

"We said nothing but what we'd seen with our own eyes," said Sholtz.

Then Millie spoke up. She said, "There are two ways of saying things. You didn't say it as if you hated to say it. You spoke as if you would be glad to see Joe Green hanged."

They all stopped working and looked as surprised as if one of the fish had jumped up and spoken. It wasn't like Millie to speak up in company: she was the silent, quiet sort.

I thought, "Millie has made an enemy of Sholtz and of Hardy." And then I thought, "It's the quiet people whom you think you can push about; but they come out strongest when you least expect it."

I looked at Millie. I could see that she was frightened at what she'd said, but she wasn't taking any of it back. Her eyes were frightened, but she stood up to them. She said, "We know that Joe never did a thing to Jeanne."

"What's that you're saying?" said old Angus, and he looked at her.

"I'm just saying that we know," said Millie.

"Just what is it you know?"

"That somebody else did it."

I'll never forget the way she said those words, and how everybody waited as if they expected her then and there to name the person. But they got no more out of her. The women shouted and the men looked at her; but Millie said nothing. She seemed to go back inside herself.

At last Angus quieted them all.

"That's enough," he said. "Whatever it is that Millie

knows, this is not the time nor the place for us to hear it. Get on with the fish now; it's getting dark, and the fog is coming in thick."

For quite a long time after that nobody dared to speak again. Then Angus said, "I'm just thinking that if there's truth in what the girl says, then Joe Green didn't do it. If that is so, the person who did it is still free, and I'm thinking that with the dark and the fog it would be wise for none of our women to go home alone." Then he looked at me: "You, boy, go along home before the dark comes."

I was very afraid when I got out onto the road. Then I decided what I would do; I would wait until I heard Millie come along with the cart: I would go home with her even if I got my clothes covered with paint and smelling of fish.

It was strange that nobody remembered Millie; she had been loading her cart with fish when Angus spoke. Nobody thought about her having to go home alone. I stood there in the fog and darkness and waited, but Millie didn't come. Others went by, two or three at a time, but I kept out of sight. The sound of their footsteps died away. It got darker and foggier. I wished that Millie would hurry.

There was a deep silence as if the fog had shut out all sounds. I listened hard, but could hear nothing. And then at last I heard the sound of those wheels which Millie never oiled. It was a very faint sound; then it came a little nearer. Then I could see a shape in the fog and I called out "Millie, Millie." The cart stopped.

"God help us!" said Millie. "I thought you were safe at home by now. Come on, get up beside me." I quickly got up into the cart. I got paint and the smell of fish on my clothes, but I didn't care about that. There was a narrow seat in front of the cart and I sat down at the side of Millie.

"I'm cold," I said.

"Just cold?"

"A bit frightened too, Millie," I said.

We went as if the Devil himself was coming after us

"That's honest," said Millie. "Here, perhaps you'd like to drive."

I was glad to drive. Millie sat beside me, but I could hardly see her face.

"Millie," I said, "What is it you know?"

"What do I know about what?"

"Who did it to Jeanne?" I said.

"I wish I knew," said Millie.

"But, Millie, you said —— you told them ——."

"What did I say?"

"You said, 'We know who did it.'"

She didn't answer. Then I said. "They all thought that you knew, and could name the person."

Millie just laughed, a strange little laugh.

Neither of us talked much after that. Then, going up the hill, the cart stopped. "Get on, Duke!" said Millie. But Duke, the horse, didn't go on.

I was just going to shout at the horse too, but I didn't, because I knew that Duke had not stopped because of the hill. Somebody had stopped him. Somebody was feeling his way back towards the cart and us. I could hear the sound of his hands trying to get a hold on the high wooden sides of Millie's red fish-cart.

Millie didn't cry out, but I heard her breath coming short and sharp. Then I felt her body move in a quick sudden act. I knew what it was. I knew by the sound that her fish knife had struck down into the wooden side of the cart. Then she took over the driving from me and she beat Duke. She kept on beating him as I'm sure she had never beaten him before, and we went as if the Devil himself was coming after us. We didn't speak, either of us, until the village lights made us feel that we could breathe again.

"Millie," I said, "do you suppose that was him?"

"Yes," said Millie, "and I only wish I'd seen him, so that I'd know."

When we passed a street light I saw her face: it was white.

She said, "Go home at once and get a hot drink and don't tell anyone. Don't tell anyone—yet. I'll go to the market and unload this fish."

I heard the cart going on down the street; I went into the house and ran upstairs. I changed my clothes. Oh dear, there was paint all down the front and they smelt terrible! Then I went down to get warm by the fire in the front room. Sophie was there.

After a time Millie came in.

I knew at once that something had happened. She was looking white and sick. When she saw me she said, "I want you to come with me now."

I didn't ask her where we were going, or why. I just went. We went past the church and the Town Hall and we came to Dr. Gunter's house with a light burning in front with his name on it. Mrs. Gunter opened the door for us.

"Yes," she said, "the doctor is in, but he's busy for the moment with someone. Will you please sit in the waiting-room?" She looked at me and then at Millie and I saw a strange look come on her face. "Why, what's the matter, Millie?" she said. "Have you cut you hand?"

Millie looked down at her closed hand, and I saw that there was blood on it. Then, as if she couldn't hold it closed any longer, she opened her hand.

Mrs. Gunter gave a cry, and I held on to the side of my chair trying not to look and yet not able to turn away.

"I am sorry to trouble the doctor", said Millie, "but I didn't know who else to go to with it. I saw it when I was unloading the fish."

You may stop reading now and try to guess the ending.
1. *What was in Millie's hand?*
2. *Who was the murderer?*
3. *"We"—Millie and who else?*

Just then we heard the side door of the house close and knew that the doctor had let the other person out. The door of the waiting-room opened and Dr. Gunter came in. If he had seen Millie and me at once, I don't suppose he would have said what he did say to Mrs. Gunter. Not seeing us, he looked at his wife and laughed, and he said, "Well, I've seen plenty of accidents to people's hands before today without the owner looking as if Death was riding close behind him. I'm surprised that a great strong fellow like Sholtz should look like that just because he's lost a finger and got some red paint on his hands."

But death *was* close behind him, with a rope round his neck.

*　　*　　*　　*

I knew why Millie might have been found on the road just like Jeanne Adams was.

And I knew why Sholtz tried to kill her.

But why did she say, "*We* know who did it?"

"We" . . . "We?" . . . Who?

5
Singing Wind

Adapted from a story by D. Sleightholme

Captain Brooke looked at the girl sitting opposite him in the railway carriage. She had a tired, young face. Her bag had the names on it of hotels all the way from New York to Eastbourne.

"Well," he said. "We are nearly there."

"Huh? Oh, yes, yes. I was miles away, dreaming." She looked hungry and tired. "I ought to have got here earlier; but you know how it is: I had to meet people and arrange things. I'm an actress, you see."

"You are going to appear here? Isn't it rather quiet here at this time of year?"

"Ah well, perhaps. But then it's the end of the season and I wanted to have a look at this place." She turned away from him to look out of the window. "I was told a lot about it when I was little."

"I will be looking out for you," said Captain Brooke. "Where are you playing?"

"I'm not playing. I'm a singer," said the girl.

The train was slowing. She stood up and reached for her bag.

"I don't know your name," said Captain Brooke.

The train passed under the bridge, and he did not hear the answer. It stopped at the station. She hurried away. He stood for a moment looking for her; then he went on.

Captain Brooke made his way straight to the address which he had been given. It was a dark, black box of a house facing the sea. He knocked.

A small man with a flat face opened the door.

"I'm Captain Brooke. I wrote to you. Are you Captain Nye?"

"No, no, I'm not Captain Nye; the Captain only has a room here. He's our lodger. Come in, sir. I've been expecting you. He knows that you're coming."

Brooke saw a woman watching him from the inner room.

"I'm glad you've come to take that old ship away," she said. "We've given that old man a home for the last twenty years, but he's never said 'Thank you' to us once. He just sits up there and treats us as if we were servants."

"Yes, Carrie," said the little man. "Perhaps we can talk to Captain Brooke later." He turned to Captain Brooke:

"Don't expect him to be pleased to see you or to speak to you—not on a night like this."

"I don't understand. Why not?"

The woman broke in again.

"He'll be listening. He won't have many more chances of doing that. The old man has sat up there and listened to the noise of the old ship's rigging* until it nearly drives me mad. He's got strange fancies, mad fancies. Thank God that will all soon be stopped."

"I've been ordered to take the ship round the coast to our place to have it broken up. That's what I'm paid for," said Brooke. "But why does he listen? What does he hear?"

"He's blind, Captain Brooke. Perhaps you didn't know that. He's blind. He sits and listens and listens for—for something that he fancies he will hear. He does it every year, just about this date."

They stopped at the foot of the stairs. They heard the noise of a door, *bang*, *bang*, *bang* in the wind. And then there was another sound, a deep note, like a note of music, rising and then falling to silence.

"Is that the ship?" asked Captain Brooke: "—the wind blowing through the rigging?"

"Yes," said the small man. "The noise drives me mad. She has lain out there for twenty years, decaying, falling to pieces. Now he can't pay for her any more and they've taken her so that she can be broken up and sold to pay what he owes them."

"Years of good money wasted," said the woman.

Their shadows went on in front of them up the narrow stairs. Then at the top the small man turned and whispered, "Remember, he won't be pleased to see you. He'll be listening in case she sings."

"In case who sings?" asked Brooke in a whisper.

The man made no answer but pointed to a door. Then he turned and went downstairs.

Brooke knocked at the door. He waited, then knocked again; and then he went in.

The room was in darkness except for a narrow line of light from the open door. The window was open with the curtains blowing out into the room, and the night filled the room with the sound of wind and rain. There was a bed in the room, and sitting upright in the bed there was an old man, bending forward.

Brooke could see the hands, big hands now thin with age, and they were moving, moving in the half-light. Brooke knew that movement: he knew that the hands were moving as if they held a ship's wheel.

"Captain Nye?"

He seemed to be looking blindly into the rain-filled darkness, and beyond that darkness to some remembered night with high, wild winds and roaring seas.

"Captain Nye," said Brooke again more loudly.

The hands were still and fell onto the bed.

"Well, Mr. Brooke?" It was a deep strong voice.

"I've come for your ship, sir. I am sorry."

"Why should you be?"

"Why should I be?" said Brooke. "Of course I must be: I am a seaman."

There was silence. Then Nye said. "She's an old ship. My father had her, then I had her. She grew old and she took all I had to give. She is all that I have now, Brooke."

"I am sorry, sir."

"You are—sorry." He laughed. "She's old, Brooke. She may never reach your place."

"I think she will."

"You've never lost a ship? Have you?"

"No."

Nye turned towards him. "You wouldn't get into trouble if she, if she—sank?"

Brooke closed his eyes. "No, I'm sorry, Captain. I can't help you."

"I want to ask you to do something for me." Nye spoke with difficulty. He was not used to asking people to do things: he was used to giving orders. "Don't take the ship away for a few more days. I only ask that. A week, perhaps. That's all I ask."

"Why? May I know why?"

"I can't tell you that."

"Captain Nye, the weather is bad now, but when it is better I must go. You're a seaman, surely you ——"

"Thank you, Captain Brooke. Forget it; forget that I asked."

"Now wait a minute."

"Please go now, sir."

The old man half-turned, and his eyes looked at him and through him, as blind eyes seem to do. Brooke saw the face grow hard.

"Will you please get out of my room, Mr. Brooke."

Brooke walked to the door. "Good night, Captain Nye."

The old man was not listening. The wind was blowing fiercely, and the sound in the rigging was high. He was whispering something. "O God," he was saying, "let her sing for me—just once."

Downstairs the small man waited. "Was I right?"

"Yes," said Brooke. "He spoke about singing."

"That's just a fancy."

"What singing?"

"A fancy. But it's not healthy, Mr. Brooke. Not healthy."

Brooke said good night and left the house. He stood and looked at the ship. He thought of her as she had once been, with fine sails driving through the seas. He stood there for a long time.

Brooke was staying at an inn near the sea.

"Well," said the innkeeper. "So she'll be going at last, eh? The old man is going to miss her."

"Yes, I think he is. Did you know him in the old days?"

"Oh yes, I knew him. I was just a young boy, starting out to sea when Nye was sailing out of here. We boys were all afraid of him. 'What!' they'd say, 'go with old Nye! You'd forget how to sleep. No rest, no quiet, just drive, drive, drive.' That's how he came to lose his wife. He was the best seaman on the coast, and he thought his ship was God. He had no love in him except for that ship."

"You said his wife?"

"Yes. She was lost off the coast of Newfoundland about this time of year. There was a storm, a terrible storm and high winds. Nobody saw her go. She'd been standing out there as she always used to do when she was afraid, and singing—singing at the wind."

"Singing?"

"Yes, she was afraid of the sea, but he took her with him and tried to teach her to love it like he did. She was small and gentle, poor thing; but she'd sing. She used to sing when the winds were blowing just to show him that she was not afraid."

"He listens. . . ."

"Oh, they've told you that, have they? Yes: he listens on wild nights. It's always the same song:

'Sweet and low, sweet and low,
Wind of the western sea.
Blow, blow, breathe and blow,
Bring him again to me.'

That's what she used to sing."

"Thank you for telling me."

"Everybody here knows the story," he said.

The innkeeper stopped; he listened to the wind. "This wind will go down before daybreak. Have a good rest. sir."

Just before daybreak the wind fell. Brooke was dreaming: in his dream there was a tall ship and the wind was singing through the rigging. He slept again and when he awoke the sun had risen on a watery world of calm.

* * * *

Brooke was looking over the old ship. Grass was growing on her. Everything was decayed, useless. She was finished as a ship.

He went below. The Captain's room was full of shadows and smelt of decay. There was a pot there containing some black things which might once have been flowers.

He pulled open some of the cupboards, looking for something which might have belonged to the sad woman who had lived here. They were empty except for a few old newspapers, a broken plate and—a woman's shoe. He was turning to go away when he noticed something. A cupboard had moved out of its place. It was a cupboard with no back to it, and behind where it had stood there was a hole in the wooden wall of the room, opening into a dark space.

He lit a match and looked in. There was a bed there, a pot of water, a plate on which there might have been food, and a handkerchief—a woman's handkerchief.

Brooke thought: "A woman could have hidden in this place, lying there in the dark, listening to the noise of the storm, the waves beating against the sides, the shouts of the seamen. Then at last the ship came to the shore, to Newfoundland; and at night, keeping to the shadows, she reached the land, and ran and ran and ran to escape from the man whom she loved and feared."

"I wonder," he said aloud.

And now Nye was living from day to day in the hope of hearing the voice of a woman whom he believed to be dead.

* * * *

It was going to blow hard that night.

Brooke could not rest.

It grew dark and the lights went on in the houses one by one. He put on his coat, and went out. Further along the road there were the coloured lights of a dance hall, and he could hear the sound of music and singing. The door of the place was open. He went in and found a table and ordered a drink.

He saw the girl at the same moment as she saw him. She saw him and tried to look away, but he smiled at her and lifted his glass. She went on singing. Her voice was young and strong. She finished her song and then came over to him and sat down.

"You haven't got many here tonight," said Brooke.

"No, not many."

"Will you have a drink?"

"Thank you," she said.

"You know," said Brooke. "you've got a voice, a strong voice, a voice which would carry a long way."

She laughed. "It would be useful on a farm, wouldn't it, for calling in the animals."

"What will you be paid here tonight? Five pounds?"

"Five pounds? No, no, not as much as that. Far less."

Brooke decided. "Sing for me—the way I tell you—and I'll pay you five pounds."

"I'll get my coat," she said.

Captain Brooke and the girl stood on the old ship. There was a half moon, and clouds moving across the sky from time to time showed the sea glimmering beyond. Above them the wind blew through the rigging and the ship seemed to shout back at it unafraid. "Stand here," said Brooke, "and sing."

"But this is silly; it's mad!" she said.

"Sing! . . . Do you know an old song, something about wind of the western sea?"

"Look!" she said

She turned her rain-wet face to him. "Why, of course,
'Sweet and low'. Is that the one you mean?"

"Yes, I think so," said Brooke, and to himself he said, "This will give the old man something to remember."

Then the girl, standing on the old ship began to sing. Her voice rose above the deep notes of the rigging, high and sweet like a silver knife cutting through the night:

> "Sweet and low, sweet and low",
> Wind of the western sea . . . . "

He listened to her. His eyes were on the dark window; his heart was beating. The voice seemed to fill the whole wide blowing night, filled his head, possessed him. He called to her:

"That will do! Stop! Stop!"

She went on singing. He ran to her and shook her arm. "Come on, you can forget the rest." Her song stopped suddenly.

"Why, what's wrong; don't you like it?"

"Come away," he shouted. Within him there was a certain strange fear. He wanted to get away.

They walked quickly away along the street.

"What's the matter?" she said.

"Nothing, nothing. You sang long enough. That's all."

"You didn't like the way I sang it. Was that it?"

"No; you sang beautifully. Here's your money." He was holding out the note. She made no move to take it.

Brooke took her arm so that she faced him. "Tell me your name."

She was looking beyond him. He watched her eyes trying to see something which was behind him.

"Look!" she said.

You may stop reading here and try to guess the ending.
1. *Why did she say "Look!" What do you think she saw?*
2. *Who was the girl?*
3. *What do you think she heard?*

Out there on the sea something was moving—a great dark shape moving fast towards the open sea. The old ship was going out to sea, out to the wide emptiness of the hungry seas.

Brooke watched. There was no way to stop the ship. There was no desire to stop her.

"There's a man on the ship!" cried the girl.

Nye was standing at his wheel, remembering the way, feeling the wind blowing from the shore on his broad back.

"That is the end," said Brooke, "—the right end".

"He shouldn't be going to sea?"

"He should," said Brooke. "He knows his way, and where he is going."

The girl turned to him and he could see the white shape of her face in the darkness. "Why did you want that song? Why did you specially want that song?"

"Oh, just say that I like it; I wanted to hear it."

"My mother used to sing it when I was a child back home in America. I used to get frightened on windy nights like this. When my mother was alive she used to sing that song to me."

The ship passed out onto the broad open waters and was seen for a moment crossing the silver path of the moon, and for a moment she was lit with silver.

"Listen!" said the girl. "Listen! . . ."

But Brooke heard nothing.

6

The Fourth Man

Adapted from a story by John Russell

It was a strange-looking boat. Its flat floor was covered with reeds* (long thick grasses) laid on flat basket-work. The boat was held up in the water by skins of animals filled with air. It had a small sail made from the same reeds.

There were four men in the boat, three of them were prisoners escaping from the island-prison, Noumea. Dr. Dubosc was once a well-known doctor in Paris, till he was found out, and the police caught him, and he was sent to Noumea. He had planned this escape. Fenay, the second man, was a thief: he was a small weak man and he thought that the doctor was wonderful. The third man was called The Parrot*; he had a very big nose, like a bird. He was very strong—a dangerous man who had killed many men in his time.

The fourth man was the man who built the boat and was now sitting at the back. He was very small, very black; he was more like a monkey than a man. The doctor found him deep in the forest in Noumea: it was a long time before he could make him understand what was wanted. Then, in a few days, he had built the boat, and promised to sail it.

The boat was now moving fast in front of a strong wind; it was pushing its way through the waves and throwing up the water over the three men.

"Where is that ship which promised to meet us here?" asked Fenay.

"It will meet us," said the Doctor. "It will be all right. This is the day which was fixed. It will meet us at the mouth of the river."

There were four men in the boat

"So you say!" answered the Parrot. "But where is the river now? Far behind us. This wind will blow us over to China if it keeps on."

"We must not stay too near to the land," said the Doctor. "If the wind changes it will blow the boat back onto the land. The forest people may still be following us in their boats."

"So far?" said The Parrot.

"Take care, Parrot," laughed Fenay. "They are still hoping to eat you." He knew how much the Parrot feared the black men of the forest.

"Is that true, Doctor?" asked the Parrot. "Is it true that they keep all escaped prisoners and fatten them?"

"No: that's a foolish story. They would rather have the money which the Prison will pay them. But I have heard that they do sometimes eat prisoners caught in war."

"Beasts! What beasts!" he said, looking at the man who was steering the boat.

The Fourth Man sat as if he was cut out of stone; his eyes were fixed upon the course in front. He did not seem to see those three other men or even to know that they were there.

"That man," said Fenay, "might steer the boat to any place he chooses, and then get the payment for us."

"You need not fear that," replied the Doctor. "He will go where I order him to go. He is a simple thing; he has the mind of a child. He has no reasoning power. I paid money to the Head Man of his people, and he sent this man to take us out to our ship. He will do what his Head Man has ordered: that is all he thinks about."

"I'm glad you think so," said Fenay. "I wouldn't trust him. What a monkey face!"

Under the heat of the midday sun, Fenay and the Parrot slept; but Doctor Dubosc did not sleep. The ship was to meet him here: that was his plan: that was what was fixed by his friends outside. And the ship was not here! Why? Was the ship near, but perhaps the men had not seen this little boat low on the water?

"Ho!" said Fenay when he awoke. "I see that we've got a flag!"

The sail had been taken down and a red cloth had been put up.

"Yes," said the doctor. "That is to help the men on the ship to see us."

"You always think of everything," said Fenay, putting his hand down into the hole below the floor where the water-bottle was kept. The water-bottle had gone!

"Where is it? The sun has cooked me like a bone."

"You will have to go on cooking."

The Parrot raised his head. "What's that? What did you say? Where's the water?"

"I have it."

They saw that he had the bottle between his knees, and their packet of food with it.

"I want a drink," said the Parrot.

"Think!" said the Doctor. "We must guard our food and water carefully. We do not know how long we shall be waiting here."

A heavy silence fell: they could hear only the quiet *creak! creak!* of the boat. They were being pushed farther and farther away from the land. Noumea was a thin blue line behind them, and on all the wide sea around them not one moving thing could be seen.

"You were sure enough when we started," said the Parrot, angrily, "but now you do not know how long it will be."

"I am still sure," replied the Doctor. "The ship will come. We must wait."

"I want a drink," said the Parrot.

"You can have your part of the water," answered the Doctor, "but when it is gone, you will get no more. You will not get any of mine, or of Fenay's."

"I want a drink."

The doctor took out of his bag a very small cup, so small that the top of a man's finger would fill it. Very carefully he poured into it a full measure. Fenay laughed at the Parrot's face as he received it. The Doctor gave the same measure to Fenay and to himself.

"Measuring it out like this," he said, "we should have enough to last for three days."

*   *   *   *

That evening they ate a piece of bread and had another measure of water. One of the three stayed on watch all through the night, and the Fourth Man slept apart, at the back of the boat.

Fenay had the last watch. When day came he was awakened by the Parrot's foot and looked up to see his angry face.

"Good-for-nothing! Will you wake before I break every bone in your body? Is this the way you keep watch?"

"Keep off!" cried Fenay, wildly. "Keep off! Don't touch me!"

"And why not, fool? Do you know that the ship could have missed us? It could have passed us again and again while you slept!"

The Doctor stood aside while they quarrelled until in the red light of sunrise he saw a knife. Then he stepped forward: "Enough. Fenay, put away that knife!"

"He kicked me!"

"He had reason. Parrot!"

"Must we all die so that he may sleep?" shouted the Parrot.

"That is finished: forget it. Things are bad enough already: we shall need all our powers. Look!"

They looked, and saw the round empty desert of the sea. The land had disappeared during the night. They were being carried away, no one could say where or how far.

No more was said. They ate a little bread and drank their measured drops of water.

The day went on. There was no wind: the sea was like glass. The sun beat down upon them and drew out every drop of water from their bodies. They got down into the water, holding onto the side of the boat, but the sea-water was like hot oil.

The Fourth Man did not join them in the water. He did not look at them. He sat with his arms round his knees, without one movement, his eyes fixed on nothing. Whenever they raised their eyes they saw him: there was nothing else to see.

"There is one person who seems to be enjoying it," said the Doctor. "I wonder what he is thinking, what is going on in his mind?"

Fenay looked at him: "Perhaps he is waiting for us to die."

They studied him as they lay in the water holding on to the boat. "How does he do it, Doctor? We have water: he has none, but look at his skin: it is fresh, and his stomach is fat."

"I have been wondering," said the Doctor. "Perhaps his body is different from ours; he is differently made."

They climbed back into the boat.

"Is there any way in which he could steal our water?" asked the Parrot.

"No," answered the Doctor. "I am sure he could not."

"Has he some hidden store? Has he a bottle or water pot hidden away?"

They went to the back of the boat where the man sat and examined it most carefully; they looked and felt everywhere. They found nothing.

The sun went down: the sky was like a red fire and their bodies seemed to burn. Night came.

They were going to fix the order of the watches, who would be on watch first; then Fenay said, "Why must we stay on watch? Is it a sailing ship which is coming to meet us, Doctor?"

"Yes."

"Then, as we have no wind to move this boat, the ship has no wind also and cannot move."

"That is so," answered the Doctor.

"Why did you not tell us that?" cried the Parrot. "Listen

to me!" He put his face close to the Doctor's. "If you keep things from us and tell us untruths, do you know what I'll do?—I shall kill you."

Fenay laughed. The Doctor began to wish that he had taken away that knife.

The third morning came. The three men sat silent; the Doctor was afraid; the Parrot was angry; Fenay was ill. Every move that the Doctor made in measuring out the water was watched with burning eyes. Only half of their store remained.

Those same burning eyes watched the Fourth Man. Their powers were weakening: he showed no sign of weakness. While they lay restless and awake at night, he slept like a child, and the next morning was in his place again, unchanged —a fixed fact and a growing wonder.

"Doctor," said the Parrot in a low voice, "is that a man, or—what is it?"

"It is a man," said the Doctor, "the lowest, most animal-like sort of man, little higher than a monkey."

"Then—what? How does he do it?"

"Perhaps he has some way of breathing or of holding his body which guards him against thirst and heat. Or perhaps there is some leaf which he eats. Who knows?"

"Can we make him tell us?"

"Impossible! I would not know how to ask; he would not know how to explain, and I would not understand him if he did."

"Then what can we do?" asked Fenay.

"Watch him! Watch him—and in the end we shall know."

"That's right," said the Parrot. "And I'm going to watch the Doctor too, and his water-bottle."

So they watched the Fourth Man; and they watched each other.

Another day came. The measure of water was cut down to half. At the sight of the bottle Fenay fell down on his

knees and cried wildly, "More! More! Give me more!" Then
he rose and threw up his arms. "A ship! A ship!"

The others turned. They saw only the unchanged emptiness of this new and greater prison into which they had
brought themselves. They turned back to Fenay and found
him raising the bottle to his mouth. He had cut the string
which tied it to the doctor's side. Even now he was drinking.

The Parrot struck Fenay a blow on the neck, and he fell
as if dead. The Doctor sprang across the body, taking the
bottle as he went. He stood there facing the killer with the
body of Fenay between them.

"Come one step nearer and I shall break this bottle over
your head. The wind must come soon; and there are only
two of us now; half of the water for each."

"I'll take my half now," said the Parrot.

"A ship! A ship!"

"I will measure it for you." He poured out a measureful. When the Parrot drank it, he filled it up again and again. ". . . Four, . . . Five," he counted. "That is enough."

But the Parrot's hand closed round his arm as he held out the fifth cupful.

"No; it is not enough." He drank the cupful. "Now, he said, "I will take the rest of it. Ha! I have fooled you at last!"

Parrot took the bottle: "The best man wins!" He raised it to drink. Then he gave a little cry and fell. He had not seen what the doctor had put in that last cupful.

"Yes," said the doctor, throwing the measuring-glass into the sea: "The best man wins!" He laughed and raised the bottle to drink.

"The best man wins," said a voice at his ear. Fenay had raised himself on one arm: he drove the knife into the Doctor's heart.

The bottle fell; the last of the water flowed down between the reeds.

*　　*　　*　　*

Some minutes (or was it hours?) later, a sound rose up from the little boat. The Fourth Man was singing softly to himself, just as he sang in the forest.

In the end the ship came.

"Ah! There they are," said Captain Jean. "They've been here all the time, not ten miles away. Get a boat over the side, officer, and bring them in."

After some time the boat came back.

"It is as I thought, Captain," said the officer. "We were too late. They are all dead; but there is a fourth man in the boat—a forest-man from Noumea."

"He'll be all right where he is," said the Captain.

You may stop reading here and guess why the man from Noumea lived when all the others died.

Captain Jean was right. As the ship turned to go to Australia, the Fourth Man put up his own sail and turned his boat back to Noumea. Then, feeling rather thirsty after doing this work, he pulled out a reed from the floor and lay face down in the place where he had always slept. Then he pushed the reed down into one of the skins under the boat and drank his fill of clean sweet water.

He had three of these remaining, built in under the floor of the boat. They were quite enough for him until he got home.

7

The Blue Scarab

Adapted from a story by R. Austen Freeman

Dr. Thorndyke is a doctor, but he does not deal with sick people; he is a detective—a man who discovers law-breakers. Dr. Thorndyke is a scientific detective; he uses science to discover law-breakers. Dr. Jervis is Dr. Thorndyke's friend and helper. Polton works for the Doctor.

*   *   *   *

Mr. James Blowgrave came to see Dr. Thorndyke in the late afternoon: his daughter, Nellie, a pretty girl aged twenty-two, was with him.

"I did not tell you anything about the matter in my letter," said Mr. Blowgrave. "I was afraid that you might not wish to deal with it, thinking that it is just a simple case of stealing. But there are some very strange things about the case. The police say that there is very little hope of discovering the thief; so I have come to ask for your help. . . . I will tell you what happened.

"It happened just two weeks ago at about 9.30 in the evening. I was sitting in my room with my daughter, looking at some things which I had taken from a small box of old papers. Then a servant ran into the room crying, 'The hut in the garden is on fire!' A glass door opens from that room into the garden. I put the things back into the box; I turned the key and put the box back on its shelf. Then I went out into the garden through the glass door, leaving the door open. The hut was on the other side of the house.

"The hut was used as a work-room and store-room. The servants were there already, throwing water onto the fire. My daughter and I helped them for about half an hour until the fire was put out. We then went back to the house, washed our faces and hands and came into the room again to go on looking at the things.

"I took the key of the box out of my pocket and went to the shelf where the box was kept. But the box was not there!

"While we were at the fire someone had come into the room and stolen it. It looked as if someone had set fire to the hut so as to get us out of the room in order to get a chance of stealing the box."

"It seems as if that might be true," said Thorndyke. "Could anyone in the garden have seen into the room?"

"Yes," answered Mr. Blowgrave; "—and anyone could easily climb over the garden wall."

"So any passing thief might have watched you through the window and taken this chance to go off with the things. Were the things in the box valuable?"

"To a thief they were of no value at all. There were some old papers and photographs, and a small box in which there was an old letter and a *scarab*—one of those little things made by the Egyptians thousands of years ago. There are letters cut on the underside. As you know, scarabs were pressed into soft wax—as a *seal*."

"Was this scarab valuable? Some are made of jewel-stones."

"It was not a real scarab: it was made of blue glass, and it had no value. The box was stolen on July 7th, and I told the police. On July 15th I received a packet with the post-mark Southampton. In it I found all the things which were in the box, except the scarab. There was also a letter. Here is the paper in which the packet was packed, and here is the letter."

He gave the paper and the letter to Dr. Thorndyke.

There was a large wax seal on the paper. The seal was covered with very small Egyptian writing.

"Was this seal made with the scarab?" asked Thorndyke. "It is very clear."

"Yes, I think so."

"You *think* so ? Don't you know what the writing was ?"

"I don't know anything about Egyptian writing, but my daughter thinks that the marks are the same as those on the scarab; and so do I."

Dr. Thorndyke looked at the letter.

Dear Friend,

    I am sending you back some things which I took by mistake, but I have kept the scarab because I may be able to sell it.

                         Yours,

                         Rudolpho.

"Who is Rudolpho ?" asked Dr. Jervis.

"I do not know," said Mr. Blowgrave. "He seems to be a strange and rather foolish person."

"Are you quite sure," said Thorndyke, "that the scarab is not more valuable than you have thought ?"

"I showed it to Monsieur Fouquet, a very learned man who has made a great study of Egyptian remains. He says that it is not a real scarab and even the writing on it is not real Egyptian writing. It is just a set of Egyptian letters put together without any meaning."

"I think, father," said Miss Blowgrave, "that you have not told Dr. Thorndyke all the facts about the scarab."

"The story is about my great-grandfather, Silas," said Mr. Blowgrave. "He and his brother, Reuben, owned a ship in which they attacked other ships. There was war at that time between England and France. They got a lot of money and some very valuable jewels from some other ship or in an attack on a town in South America. They sold the ship and Silas came to live in the house named Shawstead in which I am living now. Reuben lived in the farmhouse next to it. They divided the money between them, but they decided to

play a game of cards for the jewels: the winner of the game
would get all the jewels. They played late into the night;
Reuben won. Silas said that he had not played fairly, and
they quarrelled. Next morning Reuben and the box of jewels
had gone: neither was ever seen again. Soon after this, Silas
went to live in Egypt. There he studied Egyptian remains.
He wrote to his wife, but never came to England until a few
months before his death. Before he died he gave his wife a
little sealed packet which was to be given to his son, William,
when he was twenty-one years old. In that packet there was
the scarab and a letter. The letter is among the papers which
you have there on the table—the papers which were sent
back by Rudolpho."

Thorndyke found the letter and read it:

> Cairo
> March 4, 1833.
> My dear Son,
>   I am sending you this valuable scarab. There is
> much to be gained from the study of Egypt. Make
> it your own. Study it often. Find the body of your
> Uncle Reuben and give him a Christian burial. Bury
> him with Christian prayers. He stole from your
> father, but he shall repay.
>   Your loving father,
>   Silas Blowgrave.

"Well," said Throndyke, "have these orders been
carried out?"

"No," replied Mr. Blowgrave. "The letter seemed to
show that Silas killed his brother Reuben, and William did
not want to bring dishonour on his family. Besides, where is
the body of Uncle Reuben?"

"The letter seems to say that whoever finds the body will

be repaid; so it seems as if the jewels are buried in the same place."

"If William had found the jewels, he would not be the owner: Reuben's son would have taken them."

"Whose would they be now?"

"Reuben's grandson, Arthur, died last year. He had no children, so he left the farmhouse and most of his money to his sister's son, and he left everything else to my daughter, Nellie."

"So the jewels are part of 'everything else', and if the jewels are found they will go to Miss Blowgrave. She will be the owner."

"I have little hope of your finding the jewels," said Mr. Blowgrave, "but I would like you to find the thief who set my hut on fire and stole the scarab; and I would like you to get the scarab back. Will you do this?"

"It is a small matter," said Thorndyke, "smaller than I usually deal with; but I will do it. Leave these two letters so that I may make a more careful examination of them, and I shall want to come and see the house—perhaps tomorrow."

"Whenever you like," said Mr. Blowgrave.

"Just one question," said Dr. Thorndyke. "Who, other than you two, knows about this scarab and its story?"

"Of course, Arthur Blowgrave knew, and he may have told his family about it."

When the two Blowgraves had gone, Thorndyke said, "Will you examine Rudolpho's letter, Jervis? I will deal with the old letter and the paper cover."

Jervis dusted the letter with a black powder so as to show up any finger-prints; he also made a large photograph of it which showed up certain broken letters on the machine used to write it.

Polton made a very large photograph of the seal. Thorndyke had gone out, but he soon returned bringing with him a map on which the Blowgraves' house was marked.

He opened out the map on the table. "Here is the house,"

3

he said, "right in the middle, and that farmhouse near it is where Uncle Reuben lived."

"I don't see the need of a map," said Jervis, "if we are going to the place tomorrow."

Polton brought four photographs of the seal and put them on the table.

Thorndyke looked at the photograph of Rudolpho's letter. "Yes," he said, "the finger-prints are quite clear. That one is from my finger: that small print is perhaps Miss Blowgrave's. We must take her finger-prints and her father's tomorrow, and see if there is any other print on the letter— not mine, nor yours, nor the Blowgraves', but the thief's."

When Jervis left the room, Thorndyke was still studying the photograph of the scarab. After a time he began to write.

Then he laughed: "Ah! But Uncle Reuben was buried about 1810—not this year. So what exactly does this mean? It might mean two things."

When Jervis returned that evening Thorndyke had finished his work: he was sitting in an armchair reading the newspaper. Three careful drawings made from part of the map lay on the table; each had lines drawn across it.

"I don't see the use of making drawings from the map," said Jervis. "Why not take the map itself?"

"I don't like to spoil the map," said Thorndyke.

*   *   *   *

Thorndyke and Jervis reached Shawstead at half-past two. Blowgrave and his daughter were waiting at the door.

Blowgrave came forward to meet Thorndyke.

"It's very good of you to come," he said, "but I'm sorry to say it's too late!"

"Too late for what?" asked Thorndyke.

"I'll show you," replied Blowgrave. He led Thorndyke into the large field behind the house and went across it until he reached a place where there was a deep hole with a lot of freshly-turned earth beside it.

"That was done last night," he said. "I walked across the

He led Thorndyke into the field behind the house

field yesterday evening and there was no hole then. It was made during the night."

Thorndyke looked at the hole and laughed.

"Well," he said. "Why does that matter?"

"Whoever made this hole was looking for Uncle Reuben and the lost jewels!"

"Yes," said Thorndyke quietly: "yes, I think that is true; but he looked in the wrong place."

"The wrong place!" cried Blowgrave. "How do you know that it is the wrong place?"

"Because," replied Thorndyke, "I believe that I know the right place. But we can easily see if I am right."

Thorndyke was carrying a small bag: he put it down on the ground. He took out of it three pieces of paper—the three maps which Jervis had seen on his table.

"You see, Jervis," he said, "the use of these maps. I have made lines on each map: these lines come together at a point at which the jewels might be found."

"But why," asked Jervis, "have you got three maps?"

"Because there are three places. Number 1 is where I think the jewels are. They may perhaps be at the point shown on Map 2. Map 3 shows where someone might think they are, but in fact they can't possibly be there. Point Number 1 is among those young trees."

They moved over to the trees: there Thorndyke took a large compass out of his case.

After a time he marked a place on the ground. "There!" he said: "that is the place. We may have to make rather a large hole, as the compass is not very exact."

"I won't ask you questions," said Blowgrave, "although I don't understand at all what you are doing. You must explain what it all means when we have finished our work."

Thorndyke took off his coat and began to cut up a large square of grass: then Blowgrave and Jervis started to dig.

"Do you know how far down we've got to dig?" asked Jervis.

"The body lies six feet below the place where we are standing," answered Thorndyke. He stopped digging and looked round the field; then he looked at the farmhouse. He laughed, and began to dig again.

They went on working for about half-an-hour. The hole became deeper and deeper. Then they stopped for a rest.

"I think, Nellie," said Mr. Blowgrave, "that we would enjoy a nice cold drink."

Miss Nellie went away towards the house. Thorndyke again looked carefully at the farmhouse.

"Why do you keep looking at that house?" asked Jervis.

"I think we are being watched," he answered. "Is this field your land, Mr. Blowgrave?"

"Yes," he said. Then he followed Thorndyke's eyes. "That is Harold Bowker," he said. "He is watching us from the window of his house. He is the son of Uncle Arthur's sister. Uncle Arthur left his money and the farmhouse to him."

"So you told me," said Thorndyke.

Miss Blowgrave came across the field with a jug and four glasses. They drank, then set to work again.

Another half-hour passed. Parts of the hole were already six feet deep and they were just thinking of having another rest when Blowgrave gave a cry and held up something in his fingers. It was a bone, brown, earthy, but quite clearly a bone. He gave it to Thorndyke.

"Yes," said Thorndyke: "it is the bone of a man's foot; from the right foot. So the rest of the body lies just outside this hole—over there. We must dig carefully and see just how it lies."

He went to the place where the bone had been found and carefully cleared the earth away. Soon the rest of the foot was seen; then the ends of two leg-bones and part of the left foot.

"Now we can see how the body lies," he said. "We must dig here." He marked a line. "I think Dr. Jervis and Mr.

Blowgrave had better dig down from above and I will work outwards from here."

Jervis looked again at the window of the farmhouse. The watcher was not there.

From then on they found some new thing every few minutes—some metal parts of the shoe, a gold watch and chain, a seal. At last the whole body, except the head, was uncovered. They stopped digging and cleared away the earth carefully with their hands.

The head was uncovered; it seemed to bend forward as if it lay upon some sort of head-rest. As the earth was cleared away, a box was seen—a wooden box strengthened with iron.

For over a hundred years Reuben Blowgrave had lain there with his head resting upon the jewels which he had stolen.

"It looks terrible," said Miss Blowgrave, coming close to her father.

The silence was broken by a voice and they all looked up surprised. A young man was standing near the hole, looking angrily down.

"It seems that I have come just in time," said the young man. "I am the owner of that box; and the body is the body of Reuben Blowgrave."

"Well, Harold, you can have Uncle Reuben," said Blowgrave, "if you want him; but Nellie is the owner of the box."

"My Uncle Arthur left everything to me," he said; "so all this is mine."

"Not everything," said Blowgrave. "He left you certain money and the house; the remainder of what he owned was left to Nellie. This is what remained."

"That is not true!" cried Harold Bowker. " . . . How did you find out where he was buried?"

"Oh, that was quite easy," said Thorndyke. "I'll show you the map which I made."

Thorndyke came up out of the hole and went to his bag. He gave Harold Bowker Map Number 3.

"But this isn't the place," said Harold.

"Isn't it?" said Thorndyke. "No; of course: I've given you the wrong map. This is the map." He gave Map Number 1 to Harold. While Harold was looking at it Thorndyke put some black powder out of a bottle onto Map Number 3: then he took the photograph of Rudolpho's letter from his case and set it and the map side by side. He was looking at finger-prints.

"You still have not told me how you found out where the body and the box were buried," said Harold Bowker.

"You have played a dangerous game, Mr. Bowker," said Thorndyke, "—and you have lost. You have not only lost whatever there is of value in that box, but you will also be sent to prison as a thief—if Mr. Blowgrave wishes. On June 7th you went into Mr. Blowgrave's house and stole certain things. You sent back some of those things: but you still have the scarab."

He turned to Mr. Blowgrave: "Do you wish to send for the police?"

"No, no," said Blowgrave. "Let him give me back the scarab. I will not take the matter farther."

* * * *

About two hours later they carried the box into the sitting-room and put it on the table. With some difficulty Thorndyke opened it. At last the top of the box was raised. Inside it they saw a number of leather bags. Thorndyke opened one of the bags and emptied it into a glass. Blowgrave gave a cry, and Miss Nellie stood with wide-open eyes: the glass was full of bright red jewels, like drops of blood. In each bag they found a different sort of jewel. It was not possible to guess their value.

"But how," said Blowgrave at last, "how did you find where these jewels were hidden?"

"It was not difficult," said Thorndyke. "The seal made from the scarab gave us the answer. Silas's letter was quite clear: it said, 'There is much to be gained from the study of

The glass was full of bright red jewels

Egypt,' meaning 'If you want to find the jewels, study the Egyptian writing on the scarab.' It said, 'Find the body of Uncle Reuben . . . he shall repay'—meaning 'If you find the body you will find the jewels.' The marks on the scarab were Egyptian letters used to spell English words. That is why Dr. Fouquet could not read it: he knows very little English and he expected the marks to stand for Egyptian words. This is the meaning of the writing":

UNCLE REUBEN IS IN THE FIELD SIX FEET DOWN. CHURCH TOWER NORTH 10′ 30″ EAST. HOUSE NORTH 80′ 45″ WEST.

"Then how," asked Blowgrave, "did Harold make such a bad mistake ? Why did he dig in the wrong place ? The orders are quite clear. All he had to do was to go out with a compass, and find the place."

"But," said Thorndyke, "that is exactly what he did. But he did not know enough."

"He took a compass," said Blowgrave, "and he found the exact points which were given in the writing. Is it possible that his compass was wrong ?"

You may stop reading here and guess why Mr. Bowker did not find the place where the jewels were buried.

"No," said Thorndyke; "his compass was right, but his North was wrong. You know what a magnet* is: As you know the needle in a compass is a magnet. The Earth itself is also a magnet. The North-finding end of the compass needle points towards the magnetic north of the Earth. That Magnetic North is not the same as what is shown on maps as the North Pole. The North Pole is a fixed place on the map, but the Magnetic Pole is always changing: it is not in the same place now as it was in 1810 when Reuben was buried. So the word 'North' on the scarab might mean Magnetic North as it was when Reuben was buried in 1810, or it might perhaps mean True North. Perhaps Silas would think, 'I don't know when my son, William—or his son—or his son's son—will read the Egyptian writing, so I will use True North (which never changes).'

"So I made two maps: Map 1 shows where Reuben is if Silas used 'True North'. Map 2 shows where Reuben is if Silas used Magnetic North as in 1810. Map 3 shows Magnetic North as in this year: Map 3 shows the place where Harold Bowker looked for Reuben and, of course, did not find him. But Silas used True North, as on my map number 1."

8

The Better Way

Adapted from "The Colour of Happiness" by Patricia Sibley

An "act" is one part of the show given in a *circus* or other amusement. A group of dancers or riders give an act, and in this story Henry gives an act with his elephant.

*　　*　　*　　*

Henry went into the little bookshop in which he had worked when he was a child. Mr. Stinchcombe came running towards him spreading out his arms to welcome him.

"Henry, my boy! So the circus is back in town. Sit down and tell me everything."

"Yes," said Henry. "Yes, it's back in town. . . . I've just finished my act in the afternoon show."

"Then I can see my dear Tamara, your elephant, again! How long is it since you were here?"

"I was here about six months ago."

"Six months ago. Ah yes, I remember. That was the time of the bread-knife murder."

"Yes, that's right. There were police everywhere, but they never caught him, did they?"

"No; they think that it was a woman, possibly a French-woman who did it. But it's all forgotten now. You will have tea, won't you?"

"I'd like to, but I'm sorry I can't. I'm losing Sally, the girl who helps me in my act: I must find another one. I put up a notice and anyone who is interested is to come and see me between 6 and 7."

The circus was in a field down by the river. There was a big tent in the middle and the cages of the animals and the *caravans* in which the circus people lived were arranged in a circle around it.

No one was waiting for Henry outside his caravan. He wondered what would happen if no one came. He couldn't do an act with just one elephant, even though it was Tamara.

Then there was a tap on the door. He jumped up and saw a strange young woman. She was very small; she had a brown skin and a mass of white hair. He knew at once by that sense which had sometimes saved his life in the forests of Burma, that it was all right: his search was ended. He had found the helper he needed.

Later, after the evening show, he went to tell Tamara the news.

"Tam," he called through the glimmering summer night. She was in the far corner of a field on the river bank—an elephant standing among the wild flowers of an English field.

"Tam.' She put her trunk around his neck, and then she started to search his pockets.

"Tam, I've got a girl for you," he said softly. "She's called Marion."

In the forests in Burma Henry had lost all reason for living, and he had found it again in the shape of a very sick baby elephant. He stayed there for some years doing one sort of work and another, and all the time caring for Tamara, making her well and strong again, teaching and helping her to grow into the beautiful young elephant that she had become. At last he was able to arrange with a ship to bring her to England, and he joined the circus so as to be with her.

Tamara lifted her trunk and seemed to search the air, and then he saw someone coming towards him over the field. It was Marion.

"Have you come to meet Tamara?" he said. "Here she is."

He watched her walk slowly towards the elephant, then stop a few feet away and slowly hold out her hand:

"Hello, Tamara. Tamara, come and talk to me. Tamara."

She spoke very slowly and carefully, as if English was not her real language. Tamara seemed to look her up and down in the starlight; then she slowly put forward her trunk and began gently to move it over the girl's head and body. Henry hardly dared to breathe. Would Tamara like her? . . . She had not shown the least sign of fear; she was going to be good! Tamara liked her.

"She's going to like you, Marion."

He helped her up onto Tamara's neck then got up behind her. He thought, "What a quiet girl she is!"; and then he saw that she was shaking with silent laughter.

"Oh, this is wonderful," she said. "I didn't know that there was anything in life so strange as sitting on an elephant in a field of wild flowers under the stars."

"I'm glad you like it," said Henry. "Tell me about yourself."

"Oh," she said, "I've done all sorts of work, one thing and another."

"But you don't come from Devon, do you?"

"No, no; I've come from Ireland, from County Clare. I ran away. I'd heard so much about England I wanted to see it for myself. My parents are both dead."

It seemed very little, and there was something in her voice which was not Irish. He didn't believe this history which she had told him: he didn't believe it at all. He got down from the elephant and turned to help her. For a moment she was in his arms, small and light and warm, and then she ran away over the dark grass. Henry walked slowly back to his caravan. He did not sleep that night.

Next morning Henry went to talk with the owner of the circus. His name was Mr. Souber. He was a big man with a red face. He was sitting on the steps of his caravan drinking tea and reading the newspaper.

"I've got a girl to take Sal's place," said Henry. "I didn't have time to bring her over last night."

"That's good," said Mr. Souber. "Sal was here telling

me about the girl just a minute ago. Your new girl wouldn't sleep in the caravan with the other girls, and Sal was rather angry with her."

"Where did she sleep then?"

"Outside on the grass."

"Well, she'll get used to things, I suppose. Tamara likes her."

"Sal didn't like her hair. She says there's a mass of it and she wondered how she got it so white."

"I think it's naturally white. She comes from Ireland, and she hasn't done this sort of work before. Her mother and father are dead."

"Mm, she seems rather a mystery," said Mr. Souber. "You know I can trust your judgment; but I would like to know a little bit more about this girl."

"Oh, she's all right," said Henry.

"Bring her along to say 'Hullo' to me, just to make sure that she hasn't been in any trouble."

Henry and Marion practised the act with Tamara down on the river bank.

"I'll go through the act from the beginning to the end. It's not quite the usual act. You see, I'm trying to show Tamara's character, how she obeys me, her strength and her gentleness. I begin this way: I say 'Oh dear, Tamara, I'm not feeling at all well'". Tamara looked at him and then her trunk took the hankerchief out of his pocket and put it to his nose.

"Thank you." Then Tamara waved the handkerchief about and threw it away. She seemed to be laughing.

So they went on through the act.

"Now," he said, "I'll show you the last and best part of it."

There was a big log of wood lying on the river bank.

"Up," Henry called. "Up! . . . up! . . . up!"

Tamara walked slowly towards the log. She pretended to struggle with it: then she raised it slowly inch by inch and brought it up as far as she could above her head.

"Down . . . down . . . DOWN!" The log was thrown down, shaking the ground beneath their feet.

"Hold it!"

One great foot came down, *bang*! on the centre of the log.

"It makes an even better noise in the tent, of course. Now she does the same thing again with you, with just a little difference. I'll get Tamara to do it using the log." So once more Tamara lifted the log up, and once more it came down,

"Let me do it with her now," cried Marion

but halfway in its downward movement Henry said "Stay."
The log stopped in mid-air. Then Henry said "Gently . . .
gently . . . gently." And very slowly Tamara put the log
down on one end.

"Oh, she's wonderful!" cried Marion, jumping up and
running to her. "Let me do it with her now."

"Oh no, she isn't used to you yet. Besides most girls would
be afraid."

"You can only die once," she said. To that there was no
answer, but Henry felt he must take care of Marion: she
seemed so fearless and yet might so easily be hurt.

"We'll finish now. You must be tired and hungry. Come
and have some dinner."

Marion went to see Mr. Souber, but he got very little
from her. Two weeks passed and Souber, driven by his wife,
was getting anxious. "It's all right," said Henry. "We shall
know in time."

They moved on to the next town, and there Henry found a
book waiting for him which Mr. Stinchcombe had sent.
Inside it there was a card: "I hear you've got a new helper.
It's very hot here; I wish we could have rain. There's some
more news about the bread-knife murder. The police have
discovered the name of the man who was killed. It was
Dumondier. I hope you'll enjoy the book. Please buy some
apples for Tamara."

Why, he wondered, had Stinchcombe told him about the
murder? It was almost as if he was being warned.

He found Marion and Tamara and they set off through the
streets until they came to the river. On the other side of the
river there was wide open country.

"Can we come here every day?" asked Marion. "It's so
beautiful! All this space: so open!"

"Some people are afraid of open spaces," said Henry.

"Oh, I could never be afraid of freedom."

"I don't believe you're afraid of anything," he said.

"I shouldn't like to be shut away from all this."

"Then I shall know what to do if you are a bad girl. I shall shut you up."

She turned quickly and faced him. "No, no! Promise me, Henry! Promise you won't ever shut me up or let anybody else do it. Please, please!"

"Of course I won't shut you up," he said. "I didn't really mean it. Look at Tamara washing her back."

This sudden terrible fear was strange, this terror of being "shut up". What was the cause of it? The time had come when he must learn the truth.

"Marion, perhaps it is rather like this in Ireland—empty hills and sunshine."

"Oh, I forget."

"Come, Marion, tell me who you are and where you come from. And stop telling me untruths about Ireland: you've never been there. I can't go on working with a mystery woman. Besides Souber keeps on asking me. Tell me, or Tamara shall make you tell me."

She laughed at him. "She wouldn't hurt me. Tamara loves me."

Then Henry gave an order. Tamara picked her up. He gave another order and Tamara walked over to the river and dropped Marion into the water.

"You see," said Henry, "Tamara likes you, but she loves me, and she will do whatever I tell her; I am her master. When I first saw her in Burma she was ill and everyone thought that she would die, but I saved her and now she will do whatever I tell her to."

He went and sat down beside Marion and helped her to dry her wet hair. He wasn't angry any more. Then he took her hands in his and waited.

She looked up at him. "All right, I'll tell you. I was foolish to think that we could go on as we have been doing. My mother was English, my father was French. We lived just outside Rouen. After 1940 my father and mother hid airmen in a cellar*—a room below the ground. Then the

Germans caught them taking another Englishman to the next hiding-place along the line; but I was not caught so I went on with the work. In 1943 I was fifteen.

"I went on with the work. English airmen were sent to me, and I sent them on to the next place. Then I was caught. The Germans wanted to know where I sent men on to. To whom did I send them? If one part of the chain is broken the whole chain becomes useless. I would not tell them. Then they . . . Then they. . . ."

She stopped. Her hands fought against him as she tried to pull them away. But he held her.

"Tell me," he said. "Tell me what they did to you."

"They shut me in a cellar. It was black. . . . No, no, I can't tell you!"

"Tell me," said Henry.

"There was no light and no food; and there were rats. I was there for five days. My hair became white: it was brown before. But I got away in the end. My countrymen said that I told the Germans; so I had to run away and I came to England."

"And your father and mother?"

"They were shot. And M. Dumondier also—the next man in the chain: he was shot. That is why I try to keep it secret that I am French."

"But the war has been over for six years."

"Yes, on paper—but not in men's hearts."

Henry looked at her. Dumondier . . . Dumondier. It could not be an accident surely?

In the next town there was a strong wind and rain, and the spring of the door handle of the caravan was broken, so that he must either keep the door locked or let it swing in the wind, making a noise.

Marion came to the caravan. She said, "It's cold and wet. What we need is hot food, so I have come to cook you a real French dinner."

She began to take things out of a basket—chicken, eggs,

Suddenly he saw the knife in her hand

oil. . . . Then she took a knife and started to cut up and prepare the food. The door was swinging in the wind—*bang, bang, bang*. Henry jumped up and locked it.

"Ah! Unlock it, please," said Marion. "At once!"

"The spring is broken; it's the only way to keep it shut."

"Unlock it!" The sharpness of her voice made him look round at her.

"But why? It make a noise, and it's just getting warm in here."

She took a step towards him and suddenly he saw the knife in her hand, a small sharp pointed knife.

"Open it!" she shouted at him.

He looked at the knife, and was afraid. She was coming nearer now and there was a wild look in her eyes.

"Open it, I say!"

The rain blew against the window and the cooking-pot boiled over.

Henry said quietly, "Last time it was a bread-knife."

The knife fell from her hand.

"Did he shut you up—that other man?"

"Yes," she said.

"His name was Dumondier?"

"Jean, Monsieur Dumondier's son."

"Tell me the rest. You can tell me now."

"For six years he had been trying to find me," she said. "Then he found me. I did not know who he was. He asked me to go out with him, and we went to a house. It had a cellar. He was going to lock me in the cellar and go back to France, but I fought against him. I got away, but . . . but . . . ."

She began to move away.

"Where are you going?"

"I am going a long way away. . . ."

In one quick movement he crossed the caravan, and Marion was in his arms.

"I love you," he said. "Be my wife and we will go to some

country where there are wide open spaces and you will forget the past. You shall never, never be shut in again."

The circus moved to a big seaside place in Cornwall. Tamara was a great success. The act went very well and the people loved her.

It was the evening show. He had now come to the last part of Tamara's act. He turned to give Tamara an order; then he saw a stranger, a big man in a soft hat and a raincoat, waiting just outside—waiting for Marion, and there was a policeman standing in the shadow behind him.

Henry gave Tamara the order to lift the log. "Up . . . up . . . up! . . . Down . . . down . . .down! Hold it!" *Thump*. Tamara threw it down and put her heavy foot on it.

Then he took Marion by the hand and kissed her and gave her to Tamara.

"No one," he thought, "shall ever shut her in now. She shall not be shut in some prison with a high barred window for year after year, for life. A life of madness and terror."

He gave the order: "Up . . . Up . . . Up!"

Then he shut his eyes. "This shall be the end, the escape. She shall never be shut in!" He gave the order—to throw down and then press with the heavy foot.

"Down . . . Down . . . DOWN! . . . Hold it!"

There was a terrible silence. The onlookers sat breathless.

Then at last there was a deep "Aah!" from hundreds of voices.

What had happened? Why that delay? Why that breathless silence? Tamara had waited before obeying, and then there was that cry "Aah!" What did it mean?

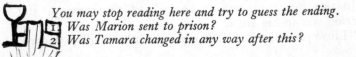

You may stop reading here and try to guess the ending.
1. *Was Marion sent to prison?*
2. *Was Tamara changed in any way after this?*

Henry opened his eyes.

For the first time ever in her life Tamara had disobeyed him. She had set Marion down on her feet. Marion stood for a moment and then fell fainting to the ground. The big man followed Henry as he carried her out.

*   *   *   *

The judge heard her story. She had killed Dumondier in self-defence. She was set free.

*   *   *   *

"But why," said Mr. Stinchcombe, "why have you changed your act? It's Marion, your wife, who now gives the orders, sitting up on Tamara's neck, and you are lifted up and put down."

"Tamara does not trust me any more. She still loves me, but she doesn't trust me. She has never allowed me to ride her since that night. . . . She isn't mine any more, she belongs to Marion."

"But you have Marion," said Mr. Stinchcombe.

"Mr. Souber, the owner, says that it makes a better act. He says it's better this way. . . . It is: it's better this way— much, much better."

9

Lady in the Dark

Adapted from a story by Victor Canning

From the other side of the road he saw the only lighted window on the third floor go black. His eyes came down to the big door, the entrance to the building. The light came warmly through there into the cold of the evening.

After a little time a girl passed through the door, stopped at the top of the steps and pulled her coat close round her. He watched her come down the steps, turn to the left and disappear along the road. He had plenty of time. He knew that she would be gone for two hours. He knew a great many things. It wasn't difficult to find out all you wanted to know so long as you took your time and were sensible.

He crossed the road. He went past the main entrance, turned the corner of the building and went in at a side door. There was a staircase there used by the servants. He climbed up to the third floor. Then he pushed open a small door. He came out into a brightly lit passage. At the end of the passage there was a door; on a plate on the door he could read "Mrs. Walter Courtenay".

He turned the handle and went in. That door was never locked when the servant was out: the old lady did not like to be locked in. If she rang for the doorman she didn't want to have to come and open the door, not at her age, not in her condition. He knew exactly the arrangement of the rooms in the flat. Four months ago the flat on the floor below was empty and he looked over it.

He crossed the hall to the door of the sitting-room. The window of this room looked out onto the street. He had seen its window when he watched, but it was not in this room that the light had gone out. The light had gone out in the servant's room on the left. This room was dark.

He went in and shut the door behind him.

A voice said, "Who is that?" It was the first time he had heard her voice, and it was very much as he had expected, a thin old voice: she was over eighty years of age. It was the voice of a lady, of a proud woman who all her life had had wealth and an easy life, rich places—all the things which he had not had. That was why she spoke in that way—"Who are you, my man?"

He said, "Never mind who I am, and don't get alarmed: I'm not going to hurt you."

He went forward and sat down on a chair by the big desk. There was a certain amount of light in the room from the street outside, and he could see her sitting there on the other side of the desk. He could see her white hair and her straight back and the gold pin in her dress. She was holding up her hands a little and he saw that she had been knitting* when he entered the room.

"Well," she said, "what do you want?"

"I want the key to your safe."

"How dare you ask such a thing!"

He felt the anger in him rise. This thing was so nearly done that he was eager to get it finished. He had lived with the thing for years, thinking it over.

"I said that I wouldn't hurt you, and I won't. I just want your key. Your servant has gone out for two hours and there is nothing that you can do."

She moved forward a little in her chair and put her knitting down on the desk, but he noticed that one hand was still playing with a long knitting needle. Perhaps this was because she was a little bit afraid. Well, that suited him. He wanted her to be afraid.

"I understand," she said. "And, when you have the key, I suppose that you will take my jewels."

eager = anxious

"That's right." He laughed. "They can give me a good life from now on."

"So you have not had what you call a "good life" up to now?"

"No, I have not."

"I see. You're that sort of young man."

"How do you know I'm a young man?"

She shook her head and her hand tapped on the soft paper lying in front of her on the desk. "I have been blind for twenty years, and that only makes it easier for me to tell some things. You have a young man's voice and you're angry. You have a lot of anger in you. You feel that you have not had the things which you have a right to have. And you are a fool to think that this is the way to get these things."

"Just give me the key. You can tell the police later that your jewels were taken by an angry young man who never went to a good school. It will be a great help to them in picking me out from about ten million others."

He pulled a case out of his pocket and lit a cigarette. "I want that key. If you won't give it me, I shall take it from that chain which you wear round your neck."

"Listen to me, young man." There was a sign of anger in her voice, and she tapped with her knitting needle on the desk calling him to order. "I do not mean to give you the key, and I advise you to leave here at once. I can give the police a better description of you than you imagine. But, if you go now, I will forget this unpleasant visit."

"You don't frighten me, and I've wasted enough time. Give me the key."

"Once more, for your own good, young man, listen to me. Go away at once. Go away and work for the things which you want. Do you think that, because I am blind, I am helpless? Of course I'm not helpless. I know already a great deal about you which would help the police if you take my jewels. You are a young man about 5 feet 10 inches in height. I can tell that from the way in which you voice comes down to me

You are wearing a bowler* hat, a round hard hat, and you are wearing a raincoat. I can hear it as you move. I am glad to know that you had the politeness to take off your hat when you came into the room, but I have noticed that you keep on tapping the top of that hard hat as you hold it on your knee. You smoke: you are smoking some kind of American cigarette, certainly not an English cigarette. You did not ask me if you might smoke."

He laughed. "It's still a description which would fit thousands and thousands of men in this country. Why do you want those jewels? You have plenty of money, and I haven't; and I'm going to have some of the things which you've enjoyed all your life."

The old lady was silent for a moment, and then she said: "You want to take my jewels because they mean money. I have never looked at them in that way. To me they are memories. They all mean something in my life. If you think that I'll give you the key to my safe so that you can walk out of here with my memories, you are very much mistaken."

He stood up. He had suddenly become angry. "You're a silly old woman. What do I care about your memories, about your past, 'each jewel a memory'." He laughed. "Well, I'll tell you what I think of your memories. There's your husband's gold watch and chain; and there's a little curl of hair from your child in the back of that diamond pin. Memories are worth nothing to me, but jewels mean money, just that. That's what they mean to me."

As he moved to go round the desk her hands shook with a rapid and angry tap-tap-tap and she said "Don't dare to come near me. Don't you dare!"

"Then give me the key."

"You fool, go away."

But he did not go away, he moved slowly round the desk and stood at her side. If it had to be that way, well that's how it had to be! He had come too far, dreamt too long of this to back away now. Even so, there was something in him which

He caught her arms and held them

drew back at the thought of using force on such an old woman. She turned in her seat to face him. "Come on, give me the key," he said. "You've got no choice." He put out his cigarette and put the end of it carefully in his pocket.

But she shook her head. "I will do nothing to help you, nothing."

He found the picture which covered the safe

He stepped towards her. He put out his hands and took her by the shoulder. She struck at his hand with a knitting needle. He caught her arms and held them with one hand, while his free hand went to her neck, searching for the chain. He pulled it free. It was then that he heard her give a little cry, and her body fell back from him pulling at the hand with which he held her arms. She was lying back in the chair. He let go of her arms: she made no move.

He stood there for a moment undecided. She was an old lady. He'd never meant it this way. It couldn't be true! She couldn't be dead! She'd be all right in a few moments.

He went to the wall and found the picture which covered the safe. Nothing could be allowed to stop him now, not after all these weeks of work, listening to the servant talking to her friend in the café three miles from here where she went on her night off. He learnt that the safe was behind the picture, and that the key was on a chain round the old lady's neck. He had done all that work to learn these things.

He put the jewel cases in the pockets of his raincoat. When the safe was empty he went back to the old lady. He put his hand on her heart. It was true; she was dead.

Well, what did it matter? He had what he wanted. She couldn't tell the police the few little things that she had learned about him.

You may stop reading now and try to guess the ending of the story. How did the police learn who this man was?

Detective Inspector Burrows walked into Albert Munster & Sons' shop. It was a small but very good-class jeweller's shop. When he was alone with Mr. Munster, Inspector Burrows said, "I believe that you did some work for a Mrs. Walter Courtenay."

"Yes, that is so. Every two years her jewellery came here to be cleaned."

"How many people in this shop dealt with the stuff?"

"There are only three of us here: myself, Mr. Brown and the man we have in the workshop who does the cleaning."

Burrows looked across at Mr. Munster. He was a very short fat man, more than sixty years of age. "No," said Burrows. "No, I don't think the description fits you."

"What description, Inspector?"

"The description of the person who last night stole Mrs. Courtenay's jewels. She was found dead by her servant."

"Dead? What a terrible thing! Poor Mrs. Courtenay. But—but, Inspector, what has this to do with us?"

"You will see." Burrows took a piece of paper out of his pocket. "What I want is a young man who did not go to one of the best schools. His height is about five feet ten inches. He smokes American cigarettes, and he wears a bowler hat and a raincoat. Does that description fit Mr. Brown?"

"No, no; he's as old as I am, and he doesn't smoke. The description fits young Grierson. He's not a bad young fellow. He has been with me for about eight years." He shook his head. "Dear me, dear me; Mrs. Courtenay dead! I can't believe it."

"Well, it's true."

"What makes you think it is young Grierson?"

"Mrs. Courtenay lived alone with her servant. She had never worn the jewels since she went blind twenty years ago. The servant has never seen them. The jewels left her room once every two years to come here for cleaning. So she knew that the thief came from your shop."

"But how could she have told you? She's dead, you say."

"She was a very brave old lady. She was blind, but not

86

helpless. She knew how to deal with young Grierson. He came in to her, and I imagine there was some talk between them while she refused to hand over the key; and while they talked, unknown to him, she was making notes about him."

Burrows looked at the piece of paper and read, "*Young man, not gentleman, height about five foot ten inches, bowler hat, raincoat, American cigarette, angry, knows jewels well, Walter's watch and chain, Edith's hair in pin. Must be from Munster & Son.*"

Burrows put the paper back in his pocket. "Yes, she was no fool. The room was in darkness. She was blind. She wrote it all down on the nice soft piece of paper on her desk. She wrote it pushing the point of her knitting needle into the paper. Wrote it in pin holes which you can arrange in sixty-three different ways. These can tell anything that a blind person wants to tell you. Braille. I think you had better send for young Grierson," said the Inspector.

"Tapping away! Just think of it! Tapping away with her knitting needle in the dark," said Mr. Munster.

It was the most expensive thing on the list

10

The Luncheon

Adapted from a story by W. Somerset Maugham

My dear boy,
I shall be coming to the city on Thursday next. It would be very nice if you could take me out to lunch or dinner somewhere.

Your aunt,

Nadia.

My Aunt Nadia was my mother's sister. She looked after us as children when my mother was ill. She was very strict, but she made no silly rules; she let us do what we liked so long as we weren't a trouble to others or a danger to ourselves.

She is quite wealthy, I believe, but she lives in a cottage in the country, with only one servant-girl to look after her and do all the work in the house. But once or twice in the year she comes to the city to buy clothes and perhaps go to the theatre.

At the time of this story I was in my first year at the University. My father had a large family, and I had only five pounds a month to live on. That ought to have been enough, but I was often in difficulties. When other fellows asked me to join them in a party, it was hard to say "No"; so I said "Yes", even if it meant going without my dinner next day. In fact, at the moment when my aunt's letter arrived, I had only twenty shillings to last me until the end of the month; but I couldn't refuse!

4

I knew of a nice little restaurant where I could get lunch for three shillings each. That would leave me fourteen shillings to last until the end of the month.

"Well," said my aunt, "where shall we go? I never eat much for lunch, just one dish; so let's go somewhere nice."

I led her in the direction of the little restaurant; but suddenly she pointed across the road to the Grand Palace. "Can't we go there? That looks very nice."

"Oh, very well, if you like it better than the place where we were going," I said. I couldn't say, "My dear Aunt, I haven't enough money to take you to that grand place. It's far too expensive: it costs far too much." I thought, "Perhaps I have enough for just one dish."

The waiter brought the list. She looked at it. "Ah!" she said. "Can I have this?"

It was chicken cooked in some French way, the most expensive thing on the list: seven shillings. I ordered for myself the dish which cost least—the cheapest thing on the list—three shillings. That left me ten shillings to last till the end of the month. No!—nine shillings, because I must give the waiter a shilling.

"Would the lady like anything while this is being prepared?" said the waiter. "We have caviar."

"Caviar!" cried Aunt Nadia. "Ah yes—those fish-eggs from Russia! Now, that would be lovely! Can I have some caviar?"

I couldn't say "No, you can't, because that will leave me only five shillings to last until the end of the month." So she had a large helping of caviar—and a glass of wine with the chicken. That left me only four shillings. Four shillings would buy enough bread and cheese for a week. But just as she finished the chicken she saw a waiter with cream cakes.

"Oh!" she said, "those cakes look very nice. I can't resist cream cakes! Just one very little one!"

That left three shillings. Then the waiter brought some

fruit: she must have some. And then, of course, we must have some coffee after such a nice lunch. That left nothing! Not even a shilling for the waiter.

He brought the bill: twenty shillings. I put twenty shillings on the plate: nothing for the waiter.

You may stop reading here and try to guess the ending.

Aunt Nadia looked at the money; then she looked at me.

"Is that all the money you have got left?" she said.

"Yes, Aunt."

"And you've spent it all on giving me a nice lunch. That's very kind of you—but it was very silly."

"Oh no, Aunt."

"You are learning languages at the University?"

"Yes, Aunt."

"What is the most difficult word to say in any language?"

"I don't know, Aunt."

"It is the word 'No'. As you grow up to be a man, you have got to learn to say 'No'—even to a lady. I knew that you had not enough money for this restaurant, but I wanted to teach you a lesson. So I went on ordering the most expensive things and watching your face—poor boy!"

She paid the bill, and gave me five pounds as a present.

"Oh dear!" she said, "that luncheon has nearly killed your poor aunt! My usual lunch is just a glass of milk."

I I

Gifts of the Wise

*Adapted from "The Gift of the Magi"** by O. Henry*

This story was written at the time when men did not wear their watches on their arms as they do now, but in their pockets, with a chain. Women had long hair of which they were very proud, and they put combs at the sides and back.

One dollar and eighty-seven cents. That was all. Della counted it three times. One dollar and eighty-seven cents, and the next day would be Christmas. She sat down and cried. Della was Mrs. James Dillingham-Young. She and her husband lived in two rooms at the top of a building in a poor part of New York. Once Jim, Della's husband, had work which paid him thirty dollars a week; but now he got only twenty. Jim and Della loved each other very much.

Della stopped crying. She stood by the window and looked out. Tomorrow would be Christmas Day and she had only one dollar eighty-seven cents with which to buy Jim a present. She had been saving every penny she could for months, and this is all she had got. She had spent many happy hours planning something nice for him, something fine and beautiful which was really worthy of Jim.

Suddenly she turned quickly round and stood in front of the looking-glass. Her eyes were shining brightly, but her face had lost its colour. She quickly pulled down her hair and let it fall to its full length.

* The Magi were the wise men who brought gifts to Jesus Christ when He was born.

There were two possessions of Mr. and Mrs. Young in which they took great pride. One was Jim's gold watch. That watch had belonged to his father and before that to his grandfather. The other proud possession was Della's hair: it was beautiful hair: it flowed down her back like a golden river.

She quickly did up her hair again. She put on her old coat and the old brown hat, ran down the stairs and out into the street. She stopped at a shop: "*Madame Sofrone, Hair-goods of all kinds*". She ran up the stairs.

"Will you buy my hair?" said Della.

"I buy hair," said Madame. "Take off your hat and let me see it."

Down flowed the river of gold.

Madame lifted the hair in her hand. "Twenty dollars," she said.

"Give it me quickly," said Della.

For the next two hours Della was searching the shops for Jim's present. She found the present at last. It had certainly been made for Jim and for no one else. It was good enough to go with his watch. In the past Jim sometimes did not like to take out his watch because it had no chain; but, with that chain on his watch, Jim might look at the time in any company.

When Della reached home she set to work to do something to her hair, and soon her head was covered with little curls which made her look like a schoolboy.

At seven o'clock the evening meal was ready.

Jim was never late. She held the watch-chain in her hand and sat on a corner of the table near the door through which he always came in. Then she heard his step on the stairs. She said a little prayer: "Please, God, make Jim think I am still pretty." The door opened and Jim came in. He looked very thin and serious. Poor fellow, he was only twenty-two. He needed a new coat.

Jim stopped inside the door and stood there. His eyes

were fixed on Della. There was a strange look in them. It was not anger, nor surprise. Della could not understand that strange look. He simply stood there looking at her—looking.

Della got off the table and went to him.

"Jim dear," she said, "don't look at me in that way. I—I had my hair cut off and I sold it, because I couldn't have lived through Christmas without giving you a present. My hair will grow again. You don't mind, do you? I had to do it. My hair grows very fast. Say 'Happy Christmas', Jim and let's be happy. You don't know what a beautiful present I've got for you."

"You've cut off your hair?" said Jim, as if he hadn't quite understood the fact yet.

"Yes, I've cut it off and sold it," said Della. "Don't you like me just as well without my hair? I'm just the same girl without my hair, aren't I?"

Jim looked about the room. "You say your hair is gone?" he said.

"You don't need to look for it," said Della. "I tell you it's sold. It's sold; it's gone. And this is the evening before Christmas, Jim. I sold it for you. It may be that 'the hairs of my head are numbered'; but nobody could ever count my love for you. Shall I get the meal ready, Jim?"

Jim took Della in his arms and kissed her. Then he took a packet out of his coat pocket and put it on the table.

"Don't make any mistake, Della", he said. "I don't think there's anything that you could do to your hair which would make me love my girl any less. But, if you will undo that packet, you will see why I was rather surprised at first."

You may stop reading here and try to guess the end of this story.

Della undid the packet and gave a cry of joy. Then she began to cry. For there lay the combs! The set of combs, side and back, which she had looked at so long in the window of a shop. They were beautiful combs with jewels in them, just the right colour for her hair. She had looked at them and wanted them, yet never hoped to possess them. Now they were hers; but the hair for which she had wanted them was gone.

She looked up at Jim with tear-filled eyes. Then, with a smile, she said, "My hair grows so fast, Jim."

She jumped up and cried, "Oh! Oh! Oh!"

Jim had not yet seen his beautiful present. She held it out to him in her open hand. The bright gold shone.

"Isn't it beautiful, Jim? I hunted all over the town to find it. You'll have to look at the time a hundred times a day now. Give me your watch, I want to see how it looks on it."

Jim did not obey. He sat down, and put his hands behind his head and smiled.

"Della," he said, "let's put our Christmas presents away and keep them for a time. They're too nice to use just at present. . . . I sold the watch to get the money to buy your combs. Now shall we have our evening meal?"

The Magi brought presents to Jesus Christ on the first Christmas of all Christmases. They first had the idea of giving Christmas presents. They were wise. Here I have told you this story of two foolish children in a poor set of rooms who gave up for each other his or her greatest treasure. They chose their presents unwisely; but those gifts which are the sign of real love are the best gifts of all.

I2

Past and Future

Adapted from a story by Muriel A. Jemmett

Elizabeth drove her little car slowly and carefully along the narrow lane: it led to the soft lights of a little cottage which stood all alone.

She stopped outside the white gate. The bright lights from the lamps of the car showed that she had reached Belinda's place at last. Rose Cottage had not been easy to find, although Belinda had given her such careful directions.

It was October, and the evening was cold. She pulled her warm red coat round her: then she hurried up the path, carrying her case in her left hand.

What a beautiful place it was! It was so quiet! Except for the whisper of the wind and, now and again, the notes of a bird, not a sound could be heard.

There was no answer to her first knock. Then the door opened, and she had a surprise. Instead of her friend she saw a curiously-dressed woman standing in the doorway. She had a long, black dress reaching down almost to the floor. On the front of her dress there was a white cotton apron.[1] On the top of her head there was a small white cap with long white pieces hanging down her back. She looked as surprised at the sight of the visitor as Elizabeth did at the sight of her.

"Good evening," said Elizabeth. "Does Miss Hill live here?"

[1] Apron—Cloth worn by women over front of body to keep clothes clean.

She felt as if she were entering another age

The woman looked even more surprised. "No," she answered in a low voice: "this is Mr. and Mrs. Upton's house, madam."

"I was sure that this was the right address," said Elizabeth. "But I must have made some mistake. May I telephone my friend from here and she will put me right?"

The girl's surprise had changed to fear: she was looking over Elizabeth's shoulder. Her mouth was wide open; and her eyes were terrified. Elizabeth turned quickly to see the cause of her alarm, but all she could see was the head-lamps of her little car shining into the darkness and lighting up a circle of the country beyond.

Another door opened suddenly and an equally strangely-dressed person appeared. He was aged about forty. He had hair growing down the sides of his face, but no beard. He wore a curious green silk coat and a cloth was tied high up round his neck. He seemed to have very thin legs. Elizabeth thought that she must have come into a fancy-dress party—a party in which people dress up in fanciful clothes.

"Lucy! What is the matter, girl?" asked Mr. Upton. "You look frightened out of your senses. Why did you not ask the lady to come in out of the cold wind?"

Lucy did not answer, but ran away.

"Will you step this way, madam," said Mr. Upton, "and meet my wife?"

He bowed and led her into the room which he had just left. Elizabeth followed him and put down her case in the corner. She felt as if she were entering another age! The room was furnished just like a room of a hundred years ago. The table, chairs, curtains, oil-lamp—everything might have been copied from a picture in some old story-book.

A lady was sitting in a large chair near the fire. She seemed to be rather weak and ill. She said a few words of greeting as they entered the room. Her long grey dress covered her feet, and she had a light silk thing over her shoulders and a pretty little cap on her head. She was shielding her face from the heat of the fire.

Mr. Upton offered Elizabeth a chair. As she sat down she felt rather uncomfortable in her short dress, her bright red coat and heavy shoes. She had dressed for a week-end in the country. This room belonged to the age of Queen Victoria. Elizabeth felt as out of place in it as if she had come as a visitor from the moon. Who were these strange people? Were they playing some curious game? Or were they mad?

Mrs. Upton was looking at her: it seemed that she did not like what she saw and indeed was almost frightened by it. The visitor's hair was cut short! And it was arranged in a strange, very careless way! That red coat! Then her eyes travelled down to Elizabeth's knees—and legs. Legs! With nothing on them, nothing to hide them! She fell back in her chair with a cry—as if she had fainted.

Her husband hurried to her side.

"Now, now! My love!" he said. "Do not be afraid. This young lady is looking for her friend's house and needs our help."

Then he turned to Elizabeth: "We came here from London six years ago because of my wife's health and have had few visitors. Allow me to offer you a glass of wine."

Elizabeth thanked him. "Here's to you! Cheers!" she said, as she drank it.

Mrs. Upton closed her eyes.

"Pray forgive us for showing some surprise," said Mr. Upton. "Your appearance and way of speaking are so different from anything we have known."

These people not only looked, but behaved in a Victorian way: it was as if they were really living in the time of Queen Victoria.

"Is there some other Rose Cottage near here?" asked Elizabeth. "I've come from London this afternoon; but I couldn't get away till after five o'clock, and now it's nearly eight. I must 'phone and find out where her cottage is and tell her that I'm on my way."

Mr. Upton was looking as frightened as his wife.

"Did I understand you to say that you have come from London—a distance of over a hundred miles—since five o'clock *this* afternoon? One hundred miles in less than three hours?"

"Yes, I got delayed, and my car isn't running well."

White-faced and with shaking hands, Mr. Upton drew aside the heavy curtains and looked out. There was a silence.

Elizabeth felt uncomfortable. "Do you mind if I smoke?" she said. She took a cigarette from her case and lit it with her lighter.

Mrs. Upton gave cry after cry of terror. Mr. Upton was already frightened by the sight of the strange, horseless carriage and its bright lights, brighter than any he had ever seen on this earth. He now turned and saw this person drawing in smoke out of a short white stick and blowing it out of her mouth and nose. Surely she had come from some world of outer darkness!

He put an arm round his wife to protect her from evil. "Go!" he cried. "Go! Whatever you are! Wherever you came from! In the name of God, go! and leave us in peace!"

Darkness came over her and Elizabeth knew no more.

* * * *

When the darkness lifted Elizabeth found herself standing outside the door of the cottage, as if nothing unusual had happened. The bird was still singing and the wind whispered over the quiet fields.

The door opened and she saw her friend, Belinda, holding out her hands to welcome her.

"My dear, do come in. Have you been waiting a long time? I was in my bath when I heard your knock, and I came down as quickly as I could."

She looked at Elizabeth's face: "Whatever is the matter?

The door opened and she saw her friend, Belinda

You look as if you'd seen a ghost! Come in here and sit down by the fire."

"I think I've seen three ghosts."

Elizabeth held out her hands to the fire. "Oh Belinda, I can't think what happened. I was in this room only a few minutes ago when some people, some very strange people, the Uptons, were living here. It was all quite different."

Belinda was silent for a minute. Then she said, "Elizabeth, what do you know about the Uptons?"

Elizabeth told her story. When she had finished Belinda said, "I . . . I can't understand it! It's unbelievable! Before we say anything else, let's have a drink."

As Belinda poured out the drinks, she suddenly stopped and nearly dropped the bottle: "Is that your case over there in the corner of the room. I'm sure you didn't have your case in your hand when you came in. I thought you had left it in the car."

Elizabeth looked at her case. "Oh!" she cried: "it's all so strange and so frightening. I took my case into the Uptons' ugly Victorian room and I remember putting it down in that corner. What can it mean?"

You may stop reading here and try to guess the ending.

Belinda spoke quietly: "It can only mean that for a few minutes the past and the future met. It does happen sometimes. But let me tell you what I've heard about the Uptons. . . .

"Just before I bought this cottage a very old woman in the village told me about a strange thing which happened one night in October exactly one hundred years ago. The Uptons had come here six years earlier from London. Because of his wife's health they lived very quietly until this terrible thing happened. Next morning they took all their things and moved to another part of the country. Mrs. Upton was never quite the same again after what she saw and heard that night."

"What did she see? Tell me!"

"Well, this is the story. A very strange visitor arrived at the Uptons' home on that October evening. She was dressed in a bright red coat and had a very short dress, which hardly came down to her knees. Her hair was cut short. She talked quickly, strangely, using words which meant nothing to the Uptons. Outside the cottage she had left a horseless carriage with very bright lights. She said that she had come from London that same afternoon—a distance of over a hundred miles. She drew in smoke from a little white stick which she lit with fire out of a small silver box, and blew it through her nose and mouth. The Uptons were sure that she must have come from the Devil."

The fire burned up and the red light shone on their faces. There was silence.

Elizabeth waited. She knew what Belinda was going to say next.

"Elizabeth. . . . "

"Yes?"

"They must have seen you!"

List of extra words

agent	2	a person who acts for another
apron	12	cloth worn by women over the front of the dress to keep it clean
bowler	9	a round hard hat
caravan	8	a home on wheels for wandering people
cellar	8	a room (for wine etc.) below the ground
circus	8	a show of trained animals and performers
fog	4	very thick mist
jurymen	4	12 men who decide in court whether a person is guilty or not
knit	9	work wool with long thick needles to make warm clothes
magnet	7	an iron bar that attracts (or is attracted to) iron
mule	1	an animal of donkey-horse mixture
parrot	6	a bird (often brightly coloured) that copies men's speech
reed	6	long thick grass
rigging	5	ropes for a ship's sails
safe	9	a strong steel cupboard for money and valuable things
scarab	7	an ancient Egyptian precious stone shaped like an insect
seal	7	wax closing a paper and marked by a sign pressed on it when hot
stitch	2	fix a length of thread in cloth with a needle

Questions

1 *Nearer to God than Gold*

1 What did Jesse see? "A – – with – – –." 2 Describe the two killers:
1. "—— but very ——"; 2. "—— and ——." 3 What did the two men
want? 4 The lady was ——. What? 5 The Lady said, "Why do men
——?" Do what? 6 What is more important than gold? 7 What happened
to Doctor Charlie? 8 What were the two men doing? 9 What was the
short man doing?

2 *"Secret Agent"*

1 What is a secret agent? 2 What was there on the girl's arm? 3 What
races did the children have? 4 Where was Miss Rosa? 5 What was the
message? "A —— on her —— —— to dear Miss Rosa."

3 *One Thousand Dollars*

1 What did Richard love doing? 2 What did Bryson tell Richard to do
with the money? 3 What did Richard ask the lawyer? 4 What did Richard
write on the paper? 5 Who will get $100,000 if Richard has wasted the
$1000?

4 *The Red Fish-Cart*

1 Who found Joe kneeling by the body? 2 What had the jurymen to
decide? 3 Why was the trial stopped for two days? 4 Why did the men
look surprised? 5 What did the people expect Millie to do? 6 What did
Millie do? 7 What was there on Millie's hand?

5 *Singing Wind*

1 Why did the girl want to look at the place? 2 Nye had no love in him
except for ——. What? 3 What was there behind the cupboard? 4 What
did Nye's wife do when the ship reached the land? 5 Who used to sing
that song? When? 6 Who was the girl?

6 *The Fourth Man*

1 Who was the leader of the men? 2 What did the Parrot do to Fenay?
3 How did the Doctor kill the Parrot? 4 How far away was the ship from
the boat?

7 *The Blue Scarab*

1 What did the servant cry out? 2 What was stolen? 3 What was cut on the bottom of the scarab? 4 Was this a real scarab? 5 What did Arthur (Reuben's grandson) leave (a) to his sister's son; (b) to Nellie? 6 What did Jervis find on Rudolpho's letter? 7 What did Blowgrave show to Thorndyke? 8 (a) Who was watching?; (b) Who was he? 9 What did they find in the box?

8 *The Better Way*

1 What did the police think about the murder? "That it was done by ——." 2 Describe the young woman. 3 How did Marion speak? As if ——. 4 Marion said that she had come from ——. From where? 5 Where did Marion sleep? 6 What was lying on the river bank? 7 What did Tamara do to Marion? 8 What did Marion do because Henry did not open the door? 9 Who was the man who Marion killed? 10 What two people did Henry see? 11 What did Henry think as he gave Marion to Tamara? 12 What sound did the people make? 13 What did the Judge say?

9 *Lady in the Dark*

1 How long will the girl be away? 2 Why did he know the arrangement of rooms? 3 What had she been doing? 4 How did she strike at him? 5 Where was the safe?

10 *The Luncheon*

1 What would lunch cost at the little restaurant? 2 Where did we go for lunch? 3 What did my aunt's dish cost? 4 What did my dish cost? 5 What else did she have, besides the caviar and the chicken? ——(a)——, and ——(b)——. 6 How much was the bill? 7 What is the most difficult word to say in any language?

11 *Gifts of the Wise*

1 What did Della want to do? 2 How much was Della paid for her hair?
3 What did Della hold in her hand? 4 What things were in the packet?

12 *Past and Future*

1 What was the name of the cottage? 2 Elizabeth asked if she might ——. Might do what? 3 Where did Elizabeth put her case? 4 Why had the Uptons come there from London? 5 Who opened the door? 6 When did the terrible thing happen to the Uptons?